# The Lord Reigns

# The Lord Reigns

## A Theological Handbook
## to the Psalms

## James Luther Mays

Westminster John Knox Press
Louisville, Kentucky

*Book design by Drew Stevens*
*Cover design by Tanya R. Hahn*

*First edition*

Published by Westminster John Knox Press
Louisville, Kentucky

This book is printed on acid-free paper that meets the American National Standards Institute Z39.48 standard. ∞

PRINTED IN THE UNITED STATES OF AMERICA

94 95 96 97 98 99 00 01 02 03 — 10 9 8 7 6 5 4 3 2 1

**Library of Congress Cataloging-in-Publication Data**

Mays, James Luther, date.
    The Lord reigns : a theological handbook to the Psalms / James
Luther Mays. — 1st ed.
        p.      cm.
    Includes bibliographical references and index.
    ISBN 0-664-25558-2 (alk. paper)
    1. Bible. O.T. Psalms—Liturgical use.   2. Bible. O.T. Psalms—
Criticism, interpretation, etc.   I. Title.   II. Series.
    BS1435.M37    1994
    223'.206—dc20
                                                            94-10407

For my sisters
Sarah Mays Cannon
and
Sarah Doris Boyd

Excellent women
who love the Psalms

# Contents

# Preface

The psalms are scripture and liturgy. In every era of the church's life the psalms have been studied, interpreted, and preached. They have been sung, prayed, and used for meditation. Psalmody is a significant feature of the continuity and unity of the community of faith. This book is an expression of the conviction that the cultivation and renewal of the use of the psalms is important for the theological and spiritual health of the church. Should it serve to offer even a modest support to the attempts being made in so many quarters to renew psalmody, its purpose will be fulfilled.

The material for the chapters of this volume was generated in two closely related contexts. Sections of it were composed originally for use in an annual seminar on psalms at Union Theological Seminary in Virginia, and others during the process of preparing the commentary on Psalms for the series Interpretation: A Bible Commentary for Teaching and Preaching. Because of its relation to that commentary, this volume can be used as a companion and supplement to it. The material is designed, first of all, for theological students and ministers as a resource in their work of interpreting and using the psalms. But I hope and have reason to believe that the material can be useful to an even wider audience, those who love and use the psalms in spiritual disciplines and public worship.

The approach followed in all the chapters is theological, in the sense that the use of the psalms as prayer and praise and scripture in the church is a constant factor in the discussion. The questions pursued and goals sought are set primarily by the praxis of the devotional, liturgical, and confessional life. The critical-historical study of the psalms is put in service of the interpretation and appropriation of that praxis. An attempt is made throughout to keep the history of the use of the psalms in view as well as the history of the original composition. The chapters are thus not organized around the usual questions of critical scholarship. The focus of the volume is rather on problems and possibilities that arise in the continuing use of psalms as scripture and liturgy.

The arrangement of the chapters reflects the functions or purposes of psalmic language and literature. Judged by their literary form, psalms were composed for the most part for prayer or praise or instruction. There are a scattered number of psalms whose content makes them important testimony to the Messiah, a topic of prime importance in the use of psalms in the New Testament. All the psalms together, it will be claimed in the first chapters, comprise the scriptural liturgical language given those who by faith undertake to live in and hope for the kingdom of the LORD. So the book begins with a section on psalms as the liturgy of the kingdom of God. Then there are sections on prayer, praise, and the Messiah, each concluding with an expository treatment of a representative psalm. The psalmic function of instruction is incorporated into these three topics; the prayer psalms, for instance, serve as instruction in prayer. Instruction also is a primary topic of the essays in Part 5, whose concern is the form and function of the whole book as scripture.

The two chapters in Part 1 are interdependent. Chapter 1, "With These Words," begins with the amazing fact of the persistence of psalmody in Judaism and Christianity. For three millennia, first Jews and then also Christians have spoken of God and to God with these words. The psalms have provided a common and traditional language world, the language that speaks of the world as envisaged by faith. It is the language of those who believe in and venture to live in the everlasting, present, and coming reign of the LORD. Therein lies an explanation for the persistence of psalmody and a crucial reason for its renewal and cultivation. Chapter 2, "The Center of the Psalms," supports the first chapter by undertaking to show that the nuclear and organizing metaphor for the theology of the psalms is the liturgical proclamation "The LORD reigns." That proclamation announces the reality on which all else in the psalms depends. The chapters in the subsequent sections all assume and reflect this thesis.

The section on prayer, Part 2, is longer than the others because there are more prayer psalms than any other kind and they pose, as a group, tougher problems for understanding and use. Chapter 3, "Reading the Prayers in the Psalter," proposes a theological approach to deal with a basic agenda of interpretive questions which critical study is at something of an impasse to answer. Though a consensus is lacking with regard to historical answers to the questions of for whom and in what circumstances these prayers were originally composed, insight into how to read and use them may be found in the theological and paradigmatic types that lie in the texts themselves. It is the theological and typical characteristics of the prayers that make them portable. Chapter 4, "Means of Grace," seeks to identify and describe some of the ways in which the prayer psalms have served the practice of prayer across the centuries. Chapter 5, "A Question of Identity," is an exploration of the christological, corporate, typical hermeneutics by which psalmic prayers have been understood and used in the Christian tradition of prayer. It reflects on the question of whether that hermeneutics may not still have much to offer. In chapter 6, Psalm 13 is selected for exposition because of its typicality, which makes its interpretation illustrative for so many other prayer psalms.

In contrast to the prayers, the hymns of praise pose fewer interpretive problems and are easier to appropriate directly. Psalm 100 is used as the "text" for both chapters in the section on praise, Part 3. In form, vocabulary, and thought it is so representative of the other "imperative hymns" in the Psalter that it can serve as an entry into the entire subject. Chapter 7, "Praise Is Fitting," seeks to read the hymns that are themselves praise as a torah of praise that gives instruction about the character of praise that is "fitting." Simple unconsidered recitation of the psalmic hymns will not achieve that fitting praise which their theology intends. The psalms must be taken as scriptural instruction that gives serious guidance on the character and performance of praise. Studied as well as used, the psalms of praise can create the character and performance of praise that glorifies the LORD as god. Chapter 8, "Worship, World, and Power," develops the exegetical foundations for the preceding chapter and also illustrates how exegesis can be a search for and a listening to the instruction in psalmic hymns.

The connection between the psalms and David is one of their most obvious literary features. The connection, moreover, has been a significant factor in the making of the Psalter, the tradition about the scriptural context of the psalms, and the understanding of the figure of the Messiah. But the connection has been virtually dissolved by historical assessment of the psalms. The result has largely been to leave the David connection without serious attention and to isolate the messianic question as a matter of dependence on ancient Near Eastern royal ideologies. The three chapters in Part 4 are attempts to make a fresh assessment of the connections, each from a somewhat different perspective. Chapter 9, "The David of the Psalms," examines the connection in the three areas of the Old Testament in which the connection is presented: Samuel, Chronicles, and Psalms. Chapter 10 tries to discern the "Portrayal of the Messiah" that can be seen when the psalms that concern the Davidic anointed king are read in stereoscopic depth. The interpretation of Psalm 2 in chapter 11 follows the trajectory of the text from its setting in the royal ceremonies of Israel, through its prophetic rereading, to its application to Jesus of Nazareth. The three essays uncover the depth, complexity, and richness that inhere in the David-Psalms connection. The topic is inevitably taken up again in chapter 12.

The essays in Part 5, the final section, focus on the book of Psalms and ask whether the Psalter in its entirety can be an object of interpretation. The question is a topic of growing interest among those who study the psalms. The claim is being made that the Psalter as a whole has a form and function that can be discerned and described. Because of the coherence of its shape, moreover, the book provides a context, a literary setting, for reading the psalms in their latest and final function, that of being scripture. Chapter 12, "Going by the Book," gathers up some of the findings of those who pursue this approach. Prominent among them is the conclusion that the Psalter has been shaped to serve as a torah of David that corresponds to the torah of Moses. Chapter 13 explores the ways in which the topic of torah pervades the Psalter and contributes to its theology. Chapter 14 is a case study that offers an illustration of the interpretive dimensions that emerge when a psalm is read as part of a book of scripture.

The notes to some of the chapters do not begin to acknowledge adequately the influence and help of interpreters of present and past generations. The bibliographical postscript at the end of the volume identifies some of the resources that I have put to constant use. The kind of writing that most of the chapters involve is not subject to detailed scholarly annotation. So I need to express my gratitude for the impulses and illuminations that have come particularly from the work of Claus Westermann and Hans-Joachim Kraus, and for the stimulus of conversations with colleagues such as Patrick Miller, Jr., Brevard Childs, Roland Murphy, Gerald Sheppard, Walter Brueggemann, and J. Clinton McCann, Jr., and reading their works.

Some of the chapters have been used for lectureships in churches and theological schools. I remember with particular gratitude the cordial hospitality of Iliff School of Theology, Asbury Theological Seminary, Austin Presbyterian Theological Seminary, and the Lutheran Theological Seminary in Philadelphia. Jeffries M. Hamilton, as the editor representing Westminster John Knox Press, has been an immense help in preparing the book for publication.

Many of the chapters in one form or another have been previously published in journals. Responses to them have encouraged me to collect and order them for publication in the hope that they will serve as a useful resource for studying and enjoying the psalms. Revision has been slight. In particular, the lectures have been left in the form in which they were written for presentation. Four of the chapters were published in *Interpretation: A Journal of Bible and Theology*, chapter 1 in part in 47/2 (April 1993): 117–26; chapter 6 in 34/3 (July 1980): 279–83; chapter 8 in 23/3 (July 1969): 315–30; chapter 9 in 40/2 (April 1986): 143–55. Chapter 2 appeared in *Language, Theology and the Bible*, edited by S. E. Balentine and J. Barton (Oxford: Clarendon Press, 1994), 231–46; chapter 5 in the *Asbury Theological Journal* 46/1 (spring 1991): 87–94; chapter 10 in *Ex Auditu* 7 (1991): 1–8; chapter 13 in the *Journal of Biblical Literature* 106/1 (1987): 3–12; chapter 14 in *Canon, Theology, and Old Testament Interpretation*, edited by G. M. Tucker et al. (Philadelphia: Fortress Press, 1988), 299–311; chapter 11 in part in C. R. Seitz, editor, *Reading and Preaching the Book of Isaiah* (Philadelphia: Fortress Press, 1988), 39–52.

# PART 1

# The Liturgy of the Kingdom of God

Say among the nations, "The LORD reigns!"
—Psalm 96:10

# CHAPTER 1

# WITH THESE WORDS
## The Language World of the Psalms

In his *Confessions* Augustine tells how he used the psalms in a period of retreat between his conversion and baptism. "What utterances sent I unto Thee, my God, when I read the Psalms of David, those faithful songs and sounds of devotion. . . . What utterances I used to send up unto Thee in those Psalms, and how was I inflamed toward Thee by them" (IX, 4). For Augustine it was a time of preparation for a different life, of initiation into a new existence, a period in which habits of thought, customs of practice, and feelings about self and others and the world had to be reconstituted. As part of the transformation, he was learning a new language. He spoke the psalms to and before the Christian God, who was now source and subject of his faith and life. He took their vocabulary and sentences as his own. He identified himself with the speaker of the psalms. He said the psalms as his words, let his feelings be evoked and led by their language, spoke the words that resonated in his own consciousness in concord with those of the psalms. He was acquiring a language world that went with his new identity as a Christian. It was the vocabulary of prayer and praise, the "first order" language that expressed the sense of self and world that comes with faith in the God to whom, of whom, and for whom the psalms speak.

Augustine's engagement with the psalms was not unique, but was typical of early Christianity. In his use of them, he was entering into a practice that went back to the first generations of the church. What was true for him held for the church at large. Of course, not with the same profundity and intensity. Augustine was Augustine. But his experience was representative.

There was a crucial clue to the role psalms would play in Christianity in the way they were used in forming the material of the Gospels. The psalms were a primary context in the scriptures for the titles used to identify the role played by Jesus in God's way with the world: King, Messiah, Son of God, Lord. But more important, the prayers in the psalms furnish the signifying narrative motifs for the story of his passion. In the story Jesus speaks their

3

words, experiences their feelings, undergoes their sufferings. Given this relation between the self of Jesus and the text of Psalms, it is no surprise that the church saw reason in the Gospels to use the psalms as its primal language of prayer and praise.

As Christianity spread in the early years, it seems always to have been accompanied by psalmody. If one could have visited the congregations scattered around the Mediterranean during the second century, one would have found corporate and private worship living out of this book. Psalmody was virtually a mark of the church, one of the constants that constituted the distinctiveness of this new religion.

We have to imagine what was happening to the mentality of Christians, living in the world of the Roman Empire and its culture, surrounded by philosophies and religions with their own views of self and world and the gods, day in and day out, week by week, year by year, letting the psalms put them in the presence of God and undertaking to be the ones who speak and think about self and world and God according to the psalms. The differentiating and distinguishing effect on the Christian consciousness must have been incalculable.

What was true of the relation between Christians and psalmody in the earliest centuries continued to be the case during the centuries of Christian history. The relation has been maintained in different times and practices, at different levels of intensity and intentionality. But for Christianity as a whole, it has persisted as though something essential were at stake in the relation.

— II —

Obviously, during the entire period of Christian history—and during the final stages of Israel's history—the psalms have had a double life. They have existed and been used as scripture and as liturgy. They persisted in their integrity because they were scripture. And they have been the scripture that has had an especially formative role for Christianity because they were liturgy.

It is a commonplace of modern Old Testament criticism that the psalms originated as songs composed for public and private occasions of worship. Many of the psalms were written as pieces for use in the Jerusalem Temple, before and after the exile. During the postexilic period, as part of the scripture-making and canon-forming process, a selection of collections and individual pieces was established as a fixed and eventually closed collection. The psalms became scripture. Yet their use as living liturgy continued through the period of early Judaism into the beginnings of Christianity. This ongoing double life is a major reason for the important role psalmody has had in Judaism and Christianity. The two identities interacted in a remarkable way.

The identity of the psalms as scripture had three effects on their career as liturgy.

1. Their identity as scripture established them. Quite simply, they continued, in toto, as a collection, in the first rank above all other liturgical materials. Hymn writing and prayer life were stimulated by Christianity. Periods and eras, with their fashions and styles as well as sensibilities, came and passed away. The psalms were the constant, the continuity, the common language across the ages. Along with scripture and the catholic creeds, they are a foundational component of community in the world church.

2. Their identity as scripture gave the psalms a canonical function in relation to all other liturgical material. They were the model for writing other hymns and prayers. Their forms and intentions, motifs and vocabulary, shaped the liturgical creativity of the church, sometimes consciously, sometimes in subliminal ways. They were the criterion by which other songs and prayers were judged. Other songs and prayers used in their company inevitably suffered or benefited by comparison, proved to be consonant or incoherent.

3. Their identity as scripture meant that they were studied, interpreted. Where this combination of recitation and interpretation was practiced, it protected worship from decay into rote, into empty repetition. The language of worship was constantly infused and informed with a freshening instruction about its concreteness and significance. What the texts said could inform and reform the content and consciousness of prayer and praise.

On the other hand, just as scripture affected the liturgical, the practice of psalmody affected the use of the psalms as scripture. I will name two ways in which this was the case.

1. The liturgical and devotional use of the psalms gave them a place in the life of Christians that no other scripture had. They were heard more often and on special occasions. Many Christians heard scripture only when they attended a service of worship. The Old Testament and Epistles, and even the Gospels, have traditionally been read selectively and alternately, but the Psalms were used in every service. On the high days of the Christian year certain psalms were set as *the* psalm for the occasion (e.g., Pss. 51 for the beginning of Lent, 104 for Pentecost, 118 for Easter) whereas Gospel selections were more likely to vary. Where psalms were maintained in liturgical practice, they were the scripture with which people were in most regular contact. Further, their very character gave them a priority for those who practiced a private devotional life. Witness the fact that the book of Psalms is likely to be the only biblical book to be published separately.

2. When the psalms were used liturgically and devotionally, they became the language of the people. There was the possibility—and actuality—that the people became the "I" and the "we" whose praise and prayers and meditations the psalms express. That happened directly with no other scripture. We do not just listen to them—we speak through and with the psalms. The possibility of what Hans Gadamer calls a *Horizontverschmelzung* was present, an interaction of the semantic reality of a text with one's personal

fund of meanings, in a merging of hermeneutical horizons. That happens in every occurrence of the understanding of a text, but in a quite special way with the psalms because there is an attempted merging, not only of language and meaning, but of identities.

It is this feature of psalmody that constitutes its special power and poses its central interpretive problem.

— III —

Psalmody is the use of the psalms to pray and praise and teach. When we use the psalms, we say their words. The question is whether we speak their language. If we do not, then the words are empty or perverted. It is possible to say the psalms in the same way one can learn to repeat Latin phrases, with only the slightest comprehension of their meaning. The words of the psalms are the vocabulary of a particular language world. We must by means of the psalms enter and live in that language world if praise and prayer with their words are to be authentic.

I am using the somewhat opaque term "language world" to avoid the implication that what is at issue is a language in the general sense, like classical Hebrew or Hellenistic Greek. What is at issue is not simply grammar, syntax, and vocabulary, but an interrelated set of sentences that comprise a semantic sphere and the particular understanding and rendering of "world" and "existence" expressed in them. By language is meant, not English, Russian, or Chinese, but speech that goes with a distinctive way of viewing and experiencing and acting. Loose analogies are the specializations of language that arise within a field of study for talking about things in the way specialists need to talk. They are the modulations of language that express what is distinctive about the consciousness of a subculture. All the classical religions are accompanied by a language in this sense.

The coherence and reference of the psalmic language world is based on a sentence on which all that is said in the psalms depends. Everything else is connected to what this one sentence says. It is a liturgical cry that is both a declaration of faith and a statement about reality. In Hebrew the sentence is composed of only two words: the proper name of Israel's god and the verb for becoming, being, and acting as a sovereign. The sentence is *"Yhwh malak,"* "the LORD reigns."[1] In this declaration the verb is, of course, a metaphor, but not just a metaphor or any metaphor. It is what T.N.D. Mettinger has called a "root metaphor."[2] Whatever else is said in the psalms about God and God's way with world and human beings is rooted in the meaning and truth of this metaphor. It is systemic for psalmic language.

The metaphor assigns the denotation and connotation of kingship, an institution of human social history, to God.[3] Thereupon hangs its power and its problems. It employs the historic symbol for power in human affairs and history to speak of God's way with the world. But it invites modern people to complain about the absence of the symbol from their experience or to construe the symbol in terms of their accidental knowledge of kings, or both.

Let it be said at this point, once and for all, that the use of the metaphor in the psalms is not the simple projection of what kings were and did onto the divine.[4] To understand the metaphor in that way would ignore its construal and explication by the canon of textual contexts in which it is located. *Yhwh malak* does not mean what a simplistic or reductionist reading says it means; the sentence means what its use in its canonical contexts directs and requires.

The sentence itself occurs in a relatively few but crucial psalms.[5] In those contexts the verb *malak* means more an activity than an office. It is a term for a dynamic sovereignty, a sovereignty administered in two patterns of activity. One is the pattern of ordering chaos to bring forth cosmos and world. The other is a scenario of intervening in human disorder by judgment and deliverance. The reign of God is God's activity as creator and maintainer of the universe, and as judge and savior who shapes the movement of history toward the purpose of God.

All the topics and functions of psalmic language fit into this collateral pattern of active sovereignty.[6] The *people* of God, the *place* God chooses to preempt in the world, the *Messiah* as earthly regent, and the *law* of God are the principal topics. The *prayers* are the pleas and the *thanksgivings* of God's servants to their sovereign; the *hymns* are the praise of God's sovereignty; and the *instructional psalms* teach how to live in the reign of God.

The psalms are, then, the liturgy of the kingdom of God. The integrity of psalmic speech in all its forms, praise, prayer, and instruction *depends* on the proclamation "The LORD reigns." And this is of course a *central reason why* psalmody has endured in the communities of Judaism and Christianity. The Psalter as a whole comprises a language in which God and world and human life are understood in terms of the reign of the LORD.

— IV —

Any attempt to describe this language world is likely to be abstract or reductionist. The world is the Psalter. But perhaps its contours can be sketched by attempting to compile a set of sentences that draws its profile and suggests its theological force.

One power comprehends all. Everything that exists arises from, is ordered by, is related to that power. It is not known in and of itself, but has given itself a name and manifested itself in the idiom of sovereignty. The LORD reigns in every sphere.

In the sphere of transcendence, the LORD is *the* God, God of gods, the power at work to relativize every other power to which humans grant dominion over their lives, and so to undo every idolatry.

In the cosmic sphere the LORD is "maker of heaven and earth," the power that overrules the unruledness of no existence to establish the world that exists to house and nurture all life.

In the sphere of history, the LORD is lord of nations, the power that opposes governments in their politics of force and self-assertion and draws peoples toward a dominion of justice.

In the social sphere, the LORD reigns in justice and righteousness as the power that opposes the disorder of violence, deceit, and greed and draws human beings toward an order of motive and action that makes for shalom.

In the personal sphere, the LORD is the shepherd of every soul, the supreme parent to whom every life is present, the presence from whose reach none can escape, the one whose loyal love is stronger than sin and death.

The LORD maintains rule among the peoples of the world by sovereign choice of a people, a place, a person, and a pedagogy.

The people are the congregation who have been delivered from servitude to the powers of this world to become servants of the LORD in trust, loyalty, and obedience. The people of the LORD raise the question why all people should not live under the rule of the LORD.

The place is the city of God called Zion, the location in worldly space chosen as the place of the Presence and institutional symbol of the heavenly reign. The city of God stands in contradiction to the pretensions of all human institutions that claim supremacy in human life and culture.

The person is the Messiah, the one appointed to represent the LORD's rule to the world and to use his vocation to make it possible for others to live by and under that rule. By his suffering and salvation the Messiah gives hope to those who trust their lives to the kingdom of God and disproves that other rulers and dominions represent the power that rules the world.

The pedagogy is the instruction that defines righteousness and wickedness in relationship to the LORD's reign, the law that guides into the paths of loyalty leading to life.

The reign of the LORD comprehends time. It is forever and ever. It has happened and does happen in interventions of judgment and salvation, wrath and grace. It is the horizon of time toward which history moves.

The campaign to consummate the reign of God in the world continues. Nations rage against it; people ignore and subvert it. Opposition and conflict, enemies and adversaries, are part and parcel of its present and prospect.

All who seek to live in the reign of the LORD are caught in the conflict and endure the incompleteness. The people of God are opposed. The Messiah is humiliated and rejected. The faithful are undone by hostility and done in by the powers of death.

The voices and roles in the psalms are defined by the situation of the conflicted reign of the LORD. The servants of God are those who acquire their identity by having the LORD as their lord. The enemies are their counterpart. The righteous are those who trust their lives to the reign of the LORD. The wicked are the opposite. The lowly, poor, needy, humble are those who depend on the LORD for deliverance from alienation, sin, and death. Their counterpart is made up of the arrogant, the ruthless, and the proud.

The time of the psalms is the interim. The hymns proclaim among the nations, "The LORD reigns." The prayers of the people of God are based on the confidence that the proclamation is true. The instruction lights the darkness of the present with the assurance that life and experience will ultimately vindicate the proclamation.

— V —

When you read or recite the psalms, when you pray and praise through them, you are set in the midst of this language world and led to speak of reality as it does. You are invited and instructed to experience and understand world and self, society and history, through the linguistic prism of a theological sovereignty shaped by the character of a particular god.

The dissonance of this language with the one taught by our culture, its incongruity with the sensibilities of modernity, is apparent. It is traditional, not contemporary. It works with poetry and metaphor instead of science and technique. It unites rather than compartmentalizes. It sees the world as a project in creation rather than a problem of physics. It centers on a sovereign god instead of sovereign self. Its ideas are those of monarchy rather than liberal democracy. It emphasizes the finitude and fallibility of the human rather than its autonomy, sees the human essential in trust and morality rather than psychology, thinks of the individual in terms of community rather than community as an aggregate of individuals, persists in speaking of good and evil, righteousness and wickedness, instead of values, and so on and on.

The question the psalms pose is whether we shall take this dissonance and incongruity simply as a problem about which something has to be done, or whether we find in the dissonance the power of the psalms as the language of faith. The temptation has been to respond to the challenge by turning three facts about this language into disqualifications.

First, the language is ancient. That is patently true. It is therefore thought to be disqualified as anachronistic. We learned to think like that with the rise of the consciousness of historical distinctiveness in the modern period. The church always knew about present and past, eras and periods, but its thinkers did not worry about anachronism until modernity emerged. Now the notion has been pressed so far by some that the phenomenon of the human is called in question. We have impoverished ourselves of instruction by tradition. The focus of every classic is blunted. We are increasingly isolated in the present. The church cannot yield to the arrogance of absolutizing modernity. If there are no valid transhistorical continuities, then Christianity is finished. So is every other attempt to make coherent sense of the phenomenon of the human.

Second, in the last century we learned that psalmic language is a feature of the ancient Near East, belonging not only to another time, but to another culture. The use of the great metaphor of kingship to convey a coherent view of reality arose with ancient Near Eastern religions. Israel thought with the language generated by the metaphor as an ancient Near Eastern people. That is also patently true. The whole matter is surveyed and assessed in works like Thorkild Jacobsen's fascinating *The Treasures of Darkness*,[7] where Jacobsen makes clear what a profound and sophisticated achievement this theopolitical view of reality was. But Israel made a radical adaptation of this view and its language to faith in the one god, the LORD. That adaptation became the historical clothing, the linguistic incarnation of the LORD's self-revelation. And there is a serious question whether that language can be rejected or forgotten without rupture of continuity with that tradition.

Third, the language emerged as a feature of the religion of Israel. That is true. Therefore, the language can be said to be disqualified because it belongs to another religion. Perhaps it is appropriate for Judaism and the liturgy of the synagogue, but not for Christianity. Any such reductionist assessment discounts the canonical and ecumenical role of psalmody. The psalms are not merely a product of the religion of Israel, but the canonized language of scripture for those who worship the God to whom and of whom the psalms speak. The practice of psalmody in synagogue and church is the constant expression of the common entanglement of Jew and Christian in the matter of God's way in the world, and the emblem of our common vision of world and society. The depreciation of psalmody can only loosen the ties that bind us. That would be an anomaly because the language with which the New Testament understands and speaks of Jesus of Nazareth is the language of this common vision. Without its revelatory instruction the church is left with a Jesus understood by the limits and pattern of some other vision, whose roots are somewhere else than in Israel's encounter with the LORD.

The attempt to recover and renew psalmody in our time must not be undertaken merely as an embellishment of liturgical practice. Crucial possibilities for the theological, liturgical, and pastoral life of the church are involved. The liveliness and actuality of the language of the reign of God supply an organizing milieu for all the principal topics of the Christian faith. It constitutes the basis and medium of the three primary functions of our religion—praise, prayer, and the practice of piety. It provides a way of thinking and understanding that holds the individual and corporate relation to God together. Said and sung as Christian liturgy, the language of the psalms discloses the unity of the canon of scripture. It articulates a polemic against the polytheism and paganism that go unnoticed in our culture. It establishes a critical resistance to the domination of any human politics and the apotheosizing of any ideology, including democracy. The language of the psalms puts all who use them in the role of servants to the LORD God, and so lays a basis for an ethic of trust and obedience. It opens up a realm for existence in which the dying may take hope, the afflicted find strength, and the faithful encouragement.

Mere recitation of the psalms will lay hold on none of these possibilities. If, however, in the use of psalms as our praise and prayer and scripture we are led to feel and think and decide as those who live in the kingdom of God in hope of the kingdom of God, then we might begin to grasp some of them. We might be better able to trust ourselves to the One who comes saying, "The kingdom of God is at hand." That would be the right reason for the renewal of psalmody today.

CHAPTER 2

# THE CENTER OF THE PSALMS
## "The LORD Reigns" as Root Metaphor

When the psalms are read as the components of a book of the Old Testament, the question can arise about their common relationship. What holds them together as religious texts? What makes it possible to read them, as they have been read for centuries, all together? Is there anything there in the text of the psalms themselves that furnishes common ground to reading and use of the book?

It is generally agreed that the book of Psalms is the outcome of a long and complex history of composition, revision, and collection.[1] The variety among the psalms in form, function, and relationship to different traditions is obvious and impressive. Approaches that identify and group the psalms in terms of genre and cultic and social functions have brought order, arrangement, and meaning into the variety. But these approaches tend to limit the question about commonality to some one feature or set of features that appear only in distinct groups of psalms. It is, of course, possible to disqualify the question in the face of the many types, times, and purposes that have entered into the building of the Psalter.[2]

The question is at root a question about a theology of the psalms.[3] It is in the attempt to discern and describe a theological dimension assumed by and/or expressed in the psalms in all their variety that the question has its context and motive. In terms of what understanding of God and God's way with the world can the psalms be read? In one sense of the term there are as many "theologies" as there are major religious traditions that have shaped the composition and redaction of the psalms. So to state it more precisely, and in a formulation familiar in the investigation of Old Testament theology, the question is about an organizing center, about "die Mitte der Psalmen."[4] Is there in the psalms some one central, organic characterization of God out of which all the rest unfolds and to which all the variety can be related? Do the texts themselves provide such a center and provide clues to the fabric of relations that connect and arrange the rest around this center?

12

This chapter is a proposal that an organizing center for the theology of the psalms can be found in the sentence *Yhwh malak*.[5] To select this sentence is admittedly to select an item whose translation and reference are debated.[6] Verb and syntax allow a translation of the predicate as noun, "is king," or verb, "reigns." There is also discussion about its meaning in proposed cultic contexts as the interpretive sentence for ritual action symbolizing that "Yhwh has become king." The interest and concern in this paper, however, are the literary contexts of the sentence. These contexts seem to favor an under-standing of the verb as the denotation of an active dominion as well as an office, a royal activity that has a past and present as well as a constant reality. "Yhwh reigns" thus suits the purposes of this inquiry best, though with the persuasion that no translation does justice to the complex connotations of the sentence.

On the face of it, the proposal would seem to have much in its favor.[7] The title of *melek* is frequently attributed to Yhwh in vocative address and descriptions in different kinds of psalms.[8] Much of the vocabulary used to portray Yhwh belongs to royal rhetoric. Statements of Yhwh's dominion are scattered through the psalms, attached to a variety of topics.[9] The roles of warrior, judge, benefactor, and shepherd, which belong to the human kingship depicted in the psalms, are also those of Yhwh. (One has to be careful here, however, because the model in the psalms belongs to the divine, not to the human side.)[10] Then there are some obvious integrations of major topics in psalms such as Psalm 2, where Yhwh, throned in the heavens, has set his king and Messiah on Zion, his holy hill. On the other hand, the preceding First Psalm seems not to contain any royal features or connections. The same seems to be true of many other psalms.

The procedure here will be to begin with the psalms in which the sentence occurs. These are the texts whose purpose is to speak about the declaration, *Yhwh malak*. The undertaking will be to discern their understanding of the sentence and the items and relationships and activities that are inherent in that understanding. Other psalms that contain similar portrayals of Yhwh's royal activity will be considered to see what they add to the exposition of Yhwh's rule. Then the attempt will be made to arrange the important topics and functions of the psalms under the rubrics of the features of Yhwh's reign. The concern is not with the history of the notion of Yhwh's kingship in Israel or the purpose of particular psalms or the reasons for the formation of the Psalter. The horizon is the book of Psalms as a literary context, and the question is whether there are connections and interrelationships in the texts of the psalms that point to *Yhwh malak* as an organizing center.

This study is called a proposal in all modesty. Within its limits only a scheme can be laid out and its plausibility supported with illustrative citations. The testing and use of the proposal belong to the ongoing project of interpreting all the psalms in the Psalter.

— II —

The psalms in which the thematic sentence occurs are Psalms 93, 96, 97, and 99. In Psalm 47, the subject is *'elohim*. Psalms 95 and 98 are included because of a clear similarity of form and material to the others.[11] What these psalms say as exposition of the sentence can be summarized in terms of spheres of dominion, institutions of reign, and activities of sovereignty.

*Spheres of dominion.* Yhwh's reign includes all that is. These psalms speak of four spheres which constitute all reality. First, Yhwh is ruler of the gods. He is the great God, the great King over all gods (95:3). All the other gods pay him homage as the one exalted above all others (97:7, 9).

Second, Yhwh rules over the world and all its constituent elements. His majesty is superior to the mighty waters (93:3–4). The depths and heights of earth, sea, and dry land belong to him (95:4–5). They are put in awe by his wrath (97:4–5) and rejoice at his coming (96:11–13; 98:7–9).

Third, Yhwh rules over all the nations and peoples of earth. He is king over all the nations (47:2, 7–8; 99:2), and his kingship is to be proclaimed among them (96:10, 3). Their gods are but idols (96:5; 97:6–7).

Fourth, Yhwh rules in Zion and the surrounding towns of Judah (97:8; 99:2). His righteousness and justice prevail over Jacob (99:4).

*Institutions of his reign.* These psalms speak also of institutions that have been established as the instrument, equipment, and expression of Yhwh's rule. His holy throne is a symbol of his kingship and spoken of by the psalms as a virtual synonym for it (47:8; 93:2). Two descriptions of Yhwh's throne are especially crucial as characterizations of his reign. The throne rests on a foundation of righteousness and justice (97:2), terms that are of pervasive importance in the Psalter as features of Yhwh's way with the world. Yhwh is throned on cherubim (99:1), winged creatures who symbolized storm and its role as manifestation of Yhwh's appearance to enforce his rule (see 97:2–5 and the discussion of it below). The focus of Yhwh's reign is the holy mount that is the royal footstool of the divine king, whose presence is first of all above heavens and earth (99:5, 9). On the holy mount stands Yhwh's royal house (93:5), the sanctuary with its courts (96:6, 8) where his reign is known and praised. There his royal presence is available to human beings (95:2, 6; 96:9, 13; 98:6, 9). There Yhwh's name actualizes his great and awesome holiness (97:12; 99:3) Yhwh has a people who acknowledge his kingship and whose voice these psalms express; they use a royal metaphor of king and people and call themselves the sheep of which he is shepherd (95:7). He has given his people decrees and statutes to order their lives (99:7; 93:5). His voice constantly and contemporaneously addresses his people; its medium is the material of the story of his way with them and their leaders (95:7, 8–11; 99:6–8).

*Actions of Yhwh's sovereignty.* In all these psalms, the rule of Yhwh is spoken of as a powerful, awesome, effective work that expounds the verb *malak*. It is not simply a status, an office. It is enacted, displayed, and maintained. It is always a universal, unlimited sovereignty over the world and its peoples. The spheres and institutions of Yhwh's rule are grounded and secured by this ruling action. The action is sketched in summary and formulaic language that seems to allude to more comprehensive assumed patterns. Two distinct but related scenarios appear.

The first is a cosmic scenario visible in Psalm 93. Here the element of opposition is the "many waters." By Yhwh's supreme majesty he has established his reign and the world concurrently. The stability of the world is the reality of his reign. The reliability of his decrees (the specific term for the laws that order Israel's life) and the holiness of his royal residence are themselves established in Yhwh's establishment of the world. House, decrees, and world are correlates of Yhwh's sovereignty over the primeval chaos.

The second is a historical scenario in two versions. In Psalm 47 the element of opposition is people and nations. Yhwh displayed his rule in subduing them and granting Jacob-Israel a heritage (*nahalah*) of his choice. Israel's life in their land is the work of Yhwh's rule and the display of Yhwh's kingship over all the earth. In Psalm 98, Yhwh's salvation of Israel was at once the exercise of his *hesed* and *'emet* toward Israel and the revelation of his righteousness to the nations as king; his salvific work is the form of his coming as royal judge of the world and its peoples.

The references to Yhwh's action in the other psalms of this group draw on and assume these scenarios. The two are closely related, the same royal action in different spheres, one evidence of the other. Yhwh is king as maker of sea and land and as maker of his people (95:3–7). Psalm 97:1–5 portrays the identity in which Yhwh acts against the chaos waters and in the midst of the peoples by using the traditional elements of the storm theophany to describe Yhwh as the divine warrior whose appearance overwhelms earth and its peoples when he intervenes in acts of judgment to maintain his sovereignty.

Because the judgments of Yhwh are acts to enforce his rule, the psalms give a prominent place to his work as judge. Yhwh has executed righteousness and justice in Jacob (99:4). In the social life of human beings he vindicates the faithful righteous against the power of the wicked (97:10–12). He comes to judge the world and its peoples (96:13; 98:9). Psalm 99 cites Yhwh's way with the leaders of his people as a paradigm of his royal action. Yhwh answered their cry and he forgave their failures, but he also avenged their misdeeds.

— III —

Similar descriptions of Yhwh's royal activity as the reality-defining foundation of the psalmic worldview are scattered through the psalms. In their similarity to and variations on the portrayals in the *Yhwh malak* psalms, these other descriptions confirm and expand the relation between Yhwh's rule and the components of psalmic thought. All of them involve the scenario of battle against opposition that has been overcome in a manifestation of Yhwh's reign.[12] Their various testimonies can be ordered by comparing them to the scenarios of Psalms 93 and 47. The descriptions appear in Psalms 29; 68; 74:12–17; 77:15–20; 89:5–18; 104:1–9; 114.[13]

The opposition in most cases is, as in Psalm 93, some form of the *mayim rabbim* (many waters). The particular form seems to depend on the interest of the psalm concerned. The forms range from the *mabbul* (flood) over which Yhwh is throned (Ps. 29) to sea and Jordan, who give way before Israel's exodus from Egypt (Ps. 114; compare also 77:16, 19) and include the mythic identities of the primeval ocean, Leviathan (74:14; compare also 104:26) and Rahab (89:10), and the waters of the deep (104:6–7). In Psalm 68, like Psalm 47, the opponents are kings and armies of the nations (vv. 12–14).

With respect to the outcome or manifestation of Yhwh's victory over opposition, the descriptions are more evenly divided. Four of them, like Psalm 93, focus on Yhwh as cosmic monarch and the established world as his work. Yhwh has dominion over the *mabbul* (29:10), has founded heaven and earth (89:11–12), made the whole world with its waters, times, and seasons the sphere of his majesty (74:15–17; 104:1–9), and provided a fertile land and watered earth as environment of life (104:10–23). Three of the descriptions, like Psalm 47, focus on Yhwh as god of nations and peoples and Israel as manifestation of his rule. Judah became his sanctuary and Israel his dominion (114:2). He established his rule as shepherd of Israel, his redeemed people (77:20, 15). In Psalm 68 he restored his *nahalah* as a dwelling for his flock (vv. 9–10), acquired the mount he desired for his everlasting abode (vv. 16–18) and showed himself to be the patron of the helpless and the needy (vv. 5–6).

The contexts in which these descriptions appear resist a neat separation of Yhwh's roles into the categories of creator and savior. The cosmic monarch is the source of strength and peace for his people (Ps. 29:11). Psalm 74 is a lament of the congregation appealing for saving help for Yhwh's redeemed people and Mount Zion (vv. 1–2). Psalm 89 is also a corporate lament appealing to Yhwh's covenant with David and his descendants. All the deeds of Yhwh are his marvelous works, his judgments, enactments of his reign. What happens in the historical realm is continuous with what happens in the cosmic. The raging, unruled nations are the counterpart of the raging cosmic waters. Yhwh's dominion over both is constitutive of his reign and interdependent. It is this understanding of Yhwh's rule that is the basis for the psalms that combine the work of establishing heavens and earth and the people of Yhwh in the continuum of praise (Pss. 135; 136; 146; 147).

— IV —

The *Yhwh malak* psalms and those that contain patterns similar to Psalms 47 and 93 seem to present the etiology of the psalmic situation. Of course the name Yhwh invokes and draws into consideration the entire narrative tradition of the Old Testament concerning Yhwh's relation to Israel. But when the question about the assumptions behind the prayers, praise, and poetry of the Psalms is asked of the psalms themselves, these are the texts that propose an answer. How does it come about that Israel in this land at this mount praises and prays to Yhwh as God of gods, ruler of heavens and earth, sovereign over nations, and shepherd of their way? How do they come to think and speak of their corporate and personal life in terms of the saving and judging action of the one they call "my God and my King"? In the way they unfold the components and connections of the sentence *Yhwh malak*, these texts supply an answer.

They also point to the coherence of various titles given Yhwh in the psalms. His identity and work as a divine warrior, shepherd, savior, judge, lawgiver, and benefactor all belong to his identity and work as king. They also provide the contexts that show the connections between the royal action of Yhwh and the important topics and functions of the psalms. In them Yhwh's rule is related to a special people, place, and person. The praise and prayer of the psalms are those of his people. His rule sets the conditions for their life and the life of all people. The connection of these inclusive topics and functions to the central notion of Yhwh's rule will be sketched in the rest of this chapter.

Two observations are pertinent at this point. There are three long psalms that rehearse the foundation story of Yhwh's way with Israel: Psalms 78, 105, and 106. By reason of content it would seem that they should contribute to the etiology of the psalmic situation. All three are variant refractions of the narratives sequence in Genesis–Samuel, rather than of the pattern scenario of our texts.[14] All three are instructional in purpose, and their central theme is God's instruction and Israel's obedience.

In our texts the topic of God's king, the Messiah, appears only in Psalm 89, and there the description of Yhwh's sovereignty used in the psalm does not include a mention of the Messiah. The text suggests that the scenario of Yhwh's establishment and exercise of his rule is thought of as complete without the administrative arrangement of a human regent. But in the Psalms as a collection the Messiah plays a crucial role in the reign of Yhwh. This will be considered below.

— V —

As sovereign, Yhwh has a special people. Psalm 74:1–2 states the basics of the relationship. Israel is the *congregation* that Yhwh *acquired* of old; he *redeemed* and claimed them as the tribe of his *heritage;* they are the *flock of his pasture.*

Yhwh chose and claimed, led, and established them in his royal action. As the outcome of the exodus, Judah became his sanctuary and Israel his dominion; this people became his holy location and the sphere of his rule within the world (114:1–2). His victory over sea and river disclosed his rule (66:5–7), and his victory settled Israel in its land (44:1–3; see also 68:7–10; 80:8–11; 81:10).

Israel is the *naḥalah* of Yhwh, a special possession and portion among the nations, which he has acquired by his mighty works (28:19; 33:12; 74:2; 78:62, 71; 94:5, 14; 106:40).

As the one enthroned on the cherubim, he is shepherd of Israel and they are his flock. The metaphor is both royal and pastoral. It comprehends Yhwh's work of leading and guiding and of providing a place of support (28:9; 74:1; 79:13; 95:7).

Israel's worship is a declaration to all the earth that, in his "making" them, Yhwh showed himself to be *the* God (100:3) and by their praise they summon all peoples to join in the declaration, *"Yhwh malak"* (96:10).

— VI —

As sovereign Yhwh has a special place in the world. The place (*maqom*) is given various designations that identify it as the location of Yhwh's royal presence. Zion is its name. It is called the City of the Great King, his holy hill or mountain, his abode, his dwelling. It is the location of his temple-palace, his house, tent, sanctuary. The place in the world corresponds to and represents Yhwh's throne and palace above the heavens, where he reigns as cosmic monarch (99:5; 29:1, 9–10; 11:4).

Yhwh's presence in Zion is the outcome of his royal action. The city is sign and manifestation of his dominion in the world. His relationship to it is of a piece with the scenario of his relation to Israel (68:17–18, 24–27; 74:2; 76:1–2). His identity with the place is not essential, but acquired. He chose and desired it (68:16; 132:13); he founded it (87:1). Like Israel, it is his *naḥalah* as king (68:9; 79:1). The psalms even include twice the memory that Yhwh first dwelt at another place in the land and only eventually settled on Zion; it is significant that the shift is connected with Yhwh's relation to the Davidic king (78:56–72; 132).

Yhwh is resident on Zion as the victorious divine warrior, whose dominion over cosmic opposition guarantees and promises his continuing and future dominion in the world of nations. Just as the *mayim rabbim* are subject to the one in the midst of the city, so are and shall be the raging nations (46:2–3 and 5–6). Yhwh enters the city as the glorious king who is mighty in battle (24:7–10). The description of Yhwh's victory over the kings and nations who threaten the city are expressions of confidence in the divine warrior's reign (46:8–10; 48:4–8; 76:3–6).

As the place of the royal presence, Zion is both topic and place of Israel's praise (especially 87:3; 48:12–14). Prayers appealing to "my King and my God" are oriented toward it (e.g., 5:2, 7). Memory and anticipation of the joy of being there are the pathos and motive of the pious and of pilgrims (42; 43 and generally in 120—134). The holy space is criterion of fealty for all who claim the protection and salvation of the divine King (15; 24:3–6).

## — VII —

As sovereign, Yhwh has a special person. The person is called his king, his anointed, his son, his chosen, David his servant.[15]

Yhwh's relation to David and his designation as Yhwh's king is the outcome of Yhwh's initiative. Yhwh "found" him, chose him from among his people, and exalted him to be the highest of the kings of earth. Yhwh's purpose is to have a king whose kingship corresponds to and represents Yhwh's dominion in the midst of the kingdoms of the world (89:5–18, 19–37).

His king is to be Yhwh's regent in dealing with the nations and peoples of the world. He receives power and authority over other kings and rulers as Yhwh's royal grant (2:7–12). He is to be a warrior whose strength and invincibility are a reflection of that of Yhwh as divine warrior (18:31–48; 20; 21:8–12). In conflict he depends on the intervention of the divine warrior (18:1–19). His rule will extend the claims of Yhwh's rule among the nations of the earth (Ps. 110).

Yhwh's king is to be his regent in dealing with Yhwh's people. In their midst he will represent and administer Yhwh's justice and righteousness (72:1–2; 45:6–7). His strength will be the protection of Yhwh's people (20:6–9). Yhwh's blessing upon him will bring prosperity to his people (72:15–17).

Yhwh's special person and place are together administrative provision for the execution of his rule in the world. Yhwh has set his king on Zion, his holy hill (2:6). Along with the choice of Mount Zion, Yhwh chose David his servant to be shepherd of his *nahalah*, the people of Israel (78:67–72). It was through David's career of afflictions that Yhwh's choice of Zion was carried out (132).

## — VIII —

As sovereign, Yhwh orders the lives of his people. The instrument of this ordering is named variously his law, decrees, statutes, precepts, commandments, ordinances, covenant, and word. By these various forms of the will of the LORD, his people learn and are directed into his ways and paths.[16]

Yhwh's dominion over the floods guarantees the certainty of his decrees

(94:5). Like Yhwh's throne and the earth, his precepts are established forever and ever (111:7–8). The God whose word directs his people is the same God whose word brought forth the world (33:6–9) and directs what happens in it (147:15–19).

Yhwh's law is sign and confirmation of his royal activity for and with his people. Exodus, wilderness, and settlement in the land have their consummation in a people who keep his statutes (105:45; 78:1–8). His ordinances are his unique gift to Israel, which distinguishes them from any other nation (147:19–20). His kingdom rules over all, and his steadfast love is from everlasting to everlasting on those who keep his covenant (103:17–19).

David was chosen as Yhwh's anointed king to be a shepherd to Israel, who habitually did not keep the commandments of their God (78:70–72, and 5–8). So faithfulness to the ordinances and statutes is essential to the Messiah's rule (18:21–25; 89:30–37).

## — IX —

The praise in the psalms is the voice of the servants of Yhwh (113:1; 134:1; 135:1; 145:10–13), who know him to be God of gods and Lord of lords (136:2–3). They tell of his marvelous works of creation and providence and recite his deeds of salvation for his people and for those who cry out to him. They testify to the attributes of his character shown in his activity, his goodness, justice and righteousness, steadfast love and faithfulness, compassion and graciousness. The proclamation of the reign of Yhwh occurs as the invocation (145:1) and concluding summation of praise (103:19–22; 146:10). Behind all the elements of psalmic praise is the conviction that Yhwh reigns.

## — X —

The prayers of the psalms in both corporate and individual voice are appeals to Yhwh as king and lord (*'adon*) of those who pray. The vocative "my King and my God" is used in corporate and in personal prayer (5:2; 44:4; 74:12). In both, those who pray call themselves the servant (*'ebed*) of Yhwh (27:9; 37:16; 79:2; 102:14; 116:16). The designation *'ebed* is constituted by a relationship to an *'adon*. To say to Yhwh, "I am your servant" (116:16; 119:25; 143:12) is the counterpart to declaring, "You are my Lord" (16:2).

The assumption behind all the prayers is that Yhwh's royal pleasure is found in the *šalom* of all who belong to his realm. "Great is Yhwh, who delights in the *šalom* of his servant" (35:27). All the troubles described in the prayers are disruptions and violations of *šalom*. Harm to a subject is damage to the reign of the monarch of that subject.

It belongs to the office of kingship to defend, protect, and rescue the weak from the strong and to vindicate those in the right against those in the wrong.

Those who pray present themselves as the lowly (*'ani* or *'aniyyim*), who are helpless before powerful, arrogant enemies; even sickness in the rhetoric of the prayers takes on aspects of an enemy (20:5; 40:17; 109:22; title of 102). They say to their God, "Oh Yhwh, who is like you, who delivers the *'ani* from those too strong for him?" (35:10; see also 12:5; 14:6; 68:5–6; 69:33; 82:2–3; 140:12). They also present themselves as the *ṣaddiq*, whose standing with God and community is endangered by the wicked (Pss. 5; 7; 17; 26). But Yhwh is not a god whose royal pleasure tolerates wickedness (5:4). He will support the *ṣaddiq* when the wicked afflict them (11:5; 14:5; 34:5; 37:39–40; 140:12–13).

The basic petitions of the prayers correspond to the functions of Yhwh's royal activity. The most frequent is "save," along with its many synonyms (e.g., 3:7; 6:4; 7:2; 22:21). It appeals to Yhwh to act for community and individual now, as he did in the past in the scenario of Israel's foundation story. The petition "Arise, Yhwh" invokes the divine warrior, the Yhwh of Hosts whose symbolic throne is the cherubim-crowned Ark; it is also found in corporate and individual prayer (44:26; 74:22; 3:7; 7:6). The plea that Yhwh "judge" the one who prays is an appeal to the king as chief legal officer, who must hear the case of those whose cry for justice reaches him (7:8; 26:1; 35:24; 43:1).

— XI —

The psalms with the concern and purpose of instruction base their teaching on the meaning of Yhwh's reign for the conduct of life. The predominant topic is the contrast between the way of the wicked and the way of the righteous. How the wicked and the righteous fare in the present and future, whether individuals, groups, or nations, stands under the ruling judgment of Yhwh. Instruction takes different literary forms in the psalms, but its consistent presupposition is Yhwh's royal work as judge of the earth.

As ruler of the divine council, Yhwh judges even the gods, because the wicked are not deterred from oppressing the lowly (Ps. 81). As the one whose throne is established forever, Yhwh judges the nations in their wickedness and rebukes their power as he rebuked the cosmic sea (9:4–5, 7–8, 16–17). As Israel's God present in Zion, he calls the wicked to accountability before the covenant's requirements (50:4–6, 16–23). As the one throned in heaven whose gaze examines every life, he tests the righteous and the wicked (11:4–7).

Because Yhwh has been victorious over his foes and established his kingship in Jerusalem, the righteous may rejoice, but the dissolution of the wicked is certain (vv. 1–3 as introduction to Psalm 68). His reign is reason for the faithful righteous to take hope even when the wicked are powerful (97:10–12). Just as surely as Yhwh has defeated the raging sea and nations, he will deliver those who trust him from the wicked.

Yhwh in his own time will judge the wicked and the righteous with equity (57:2–10). In the present time the wicked may scoff at Yhwh's instruction, live in arrogant, boastful self-confidence, be more numerous and powerful than the righteous, prosper while the faithful suffer. But the wicked will not prevail: their end is certain; they will be cut off sooner or later. It will be plain that "There is a God who judges on earth" (58:11; see particularly Pss. 1, 9, 10, 11, 32, 34, 36, 37, 58, 73, 75, 91, 94, 112, 119; also 14, 50, 53, 82, 146, 147).

## — XII —

To summarize: The declaration *Yhwh malak* involves a vision of reality that is the theological center of the Psalter.

The cosmic and worldly action to which it refers is the etiology of the psalmic situation.

The psalmic understanding of the people of God, the city of God, the king of God, and the law of God depends on its validity and implications.

The psalmic functions of praise, prayer, and instruction are responses to it and articulations of its wonder, hope, and guidance.

The organizing role of the declaration does not ignore or obviate the variety and plurality of thought about God in the psalms. It does announce a metaphor that transcends and lies behind the variety. It is what every reader and user of the psalms may know as the code for understanding all of them.

# PART 2

# Prayers of Need, Gratitude, and Trust

Listen to the sound of my cry,
  my King and my God,
  for to you I pray.
                —Psalm 5:2

You have turned my mourning into dancing.
                —Psalm 30:11

The LORD is my shepherd, I shall not want.
                —Psalm 23:1

# CHAPTER 3

# READING THE PRAYERS IN THE PSALTER
## A Theological Approach

"I sought the LORD, and he answered me, and delivered me from all my fears"(34:4). This report from a psalmist is a testimony to the life of prayer in Israel out of which so many psalms came. For centuries Jews and Christians have used the psalms—all of them—as their prayers. Such use of the psalms is justified by the content and formation of the book of Psalms. Prayers composed for individuals and the community are together far more numerous than are any other literary type. The formation of the book of Psalms began with a collection of psalms of David for use as a prayer book among the circles of those who called themselves the humble and thought of Israel as a community of the humble.

The three clauses in the psalmist's testimony point to the three phases of prayer found in the psalms. "I sought the LORD" points to the many prayers for help composed both for individuals and the community (e.g., Pss. 3, 4, 5, 6, 7; and 44, 74). "He answered me" can represent the thanksgivings of those whose prayers for help have been heard and for whom help has come (e.g., Pss. 18, 30, 116). "[He] delivered me from all my fears" points to the psalms that are confessions of trust made by those whose lives are lived in reliance on God's help (e.g., 23, 62, 131).

The prayers of an individual in trouble make up the core of this repertoire of prayer. There are more of them than any other type of prayer, and they precede and anticipate the other types, which assume their performance. The prayers often contain promises to offer songs of thanksgiving in response to God's help (e.g., 7:17; 13:6; 26:12). They usually make statements of trust in God, which constitute the theme of psalms of trust (e.g., 3:3–6; 4:3; 5:12). In turn the songs of thanksgiving typically refer to prayers for help that were previously made (e.g., 18:6; 30:2; 116:3–4), and the psalms of trust express a confidence that God will hear and help in times of trouble (e.g., 23:4–5; 62:6; 63:7–8). In performance and faith, the other kinds of prayer are bound to the individual prayer for help.

25

Because of this interdependent relationship, the questions that the individual prayers for help pose for the interpreter concern the other kinds. Answers to them are answers for the entire group. But the questions are difficult, and answers are not subject to general agreement among those who study the psalms. The problems concern both explanation and appropriation. Obviously, the way in which the language of these prayers is construed and understood has a significant influence on their use as scripture, liturgy, and personal prayer. The meaning of the typical language of the prayers depends in the main on decisions about the identity of the person who prays in the prayers. The interpretive questions deal with different aspects of the problem of the "I" who speaks in the prayers, the status, self-understanding, situation, and intention of the protagonist of the prayers.

Who is the psalmist of these prayers? If not David, to whom most are attributed, then what is to be made of the attribution? Is the psalmist an ordinary Israelite, or the king? Are different roles in Israel's society represented? Have the prayers as we have them in the Psalter been adapted for common and corporate use?

How are the categories used by the psalmists in describing themselves to be assessed? The speakers designate themselves by terms such as lowly/humble/poor, righteous, faithful, fearers of God. What does the use of these terms intend and imply? What is to be made of the seemingly simple and stark contrast drawn between themselves and the wicked?

What circumstances and social settings are reflected in these prayers? The need depicted in them is always urgent, the pleading insistent. Language drawn from apparently quite different areas of experience is used to describe the need, often in a montage of combinations. The problems are those of mortality and finitude, predominantly. Do different psalms represent quite different identifiable experiences and social circumstances, such as sickness, social strife, trial proceedings, ceremonies for war, and so on?

What is to be made of the omnipresent enemies, almost always a feature of these prayers? Prayer seems always to be made in the presence of the enemies. At times prayer is used against them, vehemently.

Reading the psalm-prayers and undertaking to use them as prayers will inevitably face and engage these questions. An approach is needed that follows the language of the texts and at the same time discerns in the texts the features and characteristics that render them so useful as devotion and liturgy. The approach laid out in the following discussion seeks to determine the theological characterizations of the persons in the prayer psalms. It concentrates on the formulaic and typical character of psalmic language and its capacity to be read as open paradigms and symbolizations. It is in these dimensions of the prayers that the potential of the psalms to be the continuing prayers of the faithful seems to lie. The approach proposes the following:

1. The prayers have a common *theological setting-in-life* (in contrast to a cultic or social one) that is assumed, expressed, and evoked in their language. In their enactment they create a setting in which a servant appeals to a lord. They set the one who prays in the paradigmatic metaphor of the reign of God.

2. Those who pray in these prayers cast themselves in the roles of a set of theological types, primarily the lowly and the righteous. To pray these prayers is to assume one or a combination of these identities, individually or corporately.

3. The language used to describe the needs of those who pray was generated in the experience of a span of troubles: physical affliction, social affliction, warfare. But its function in these psalms is symbolic, metaphorical, analogical, for the many forms that the human predicament of helplessness can take.

4. The enemies dramatize the adversarial nature of religious faith. To trust in the LORD as god is to be opposed by other understandings of one's identity and situation, especially in times of affliction. The enemies represent the possibility that the LORD is not God, not my God.

— II —

The prayers for help (and their associated types) have a common theological setting-in-life that is assumed, expressed, and evoked in their language. They are all the language of servants (*'ebed*) of a king to the king who is their lord (*'adon*). The prayers undoubtedly arose out of various life-threatening circumstances. They reflect in varying degrees a relation to sacral institutions, through which religion in Israel ministered to those in serious trouble. But whatever the trouble and through whatever institution it was dealt with, the prayers themselves always cast the ones who pray in the role of servants appealing to their king. Their basis is the theology of Yhwh as cosmic sovereign, who has made Israel his people and all persons in it his servants. The agenda of the prayers is the agenda of an appeal to the king by those who belong to his realm. They are a religious analogy to what the subjects of a king did when they were in trouble with which they could not cope with their ordinary resources. His subjects had the privilege and right to appeal to the king for help. Those who use the prayers are exercising that right and privilege.

The following analysis is only a précis of the reality, and deals only with the prayers for help. The texts cited are only selected illustrations. But the analysis points to a way of reading and interpreting the songs about trouble that can be employed in using all these psalms.

1. Yhwh is addressed as king by his servants.

a. Yhwh is viewed as cosmic sovereign and personal God, a combination expressed by the vocative "my King and my God" (5:2; 44:4; 74:12). As cosmic sovereign, he has the power to help in any situation. As the personal God of those who pray, he has the responsibility to hear.

b. Those who pray identify themselves as the servant(s) of Yhwh (27:9; 31:16; 86:1–2, 16; 143:2, 12). All other classifications and characterizations in the self-descriptions in the prayers are features of this status. A servant (*'ebed*) belongs to another, who is called his lord (*'adon*). "I say to Yhwh, 'You are my Lord' " (16:2). In the Old Testament vocabulary, an *'ebed* is one who belongs to another. The term is not menial or derogatory. All the officials and subjects of a king, from highest to lowest, were servants of the king. To say to Yhwh, "I am your servant" (116:16; 119:125; 143:12) is to identify oneself as a subject of his rule.

c. "Great is Yhwh, who delights in the welfare [shalom] of his servant" (35:27). The assumption behind all the prayers is that Yhwh's royal pleasure is found in the shalom of all who belong to his realm. Shalom means a wholeness and rightness of existence that has physical, social, psychic, and spiritual dimensions. All the troubles described in the prayers (suffering, accusation, alienation and hostility, dereliction) are disruptions of shalom. The lord has a vested interest in the welfare of his servant. Harm to a subject is damage to the reign of the king.

2. The character and policy of Yhwh's kingship shape the description of self and trouble in the prayers.

a. "O Yhwh, who is like you, who delivers the weak [*'ani*] from him who is too strong for him?" (35:10). It belongs to the office of king to sustain the helpless and restrain the strong from damaging the shalom of others (see 73:1–4, 12–14 on the Davidic king). Yhwh maintains that policy perfectly (140:12; 12:5; 14:6; 68:5–6; 69:33; 82:2–3). Those who pray present themselves as helpless before the threats of strong, arrogant enemies (40:17; 70:5; 109:22; title of 102).

b. Yhwh "loves righteousness and justice" (33:5). "You are not a God who delights in wickedness" (5:4). He supports the righteous (*saddiq*) when the wicked (*raša'*) afflict them (11:5; 14:5; 34:5; 37:39–40; 140:12–13). Only the righteous have standing before him (15; 24:3–6). Those who pray often present themselves as the ones innocent (*saddiq*) in a situation in which they are beset by those guilty (*raša'*) of destroying shalom and opposing the ways of God (Pss. 5; 7; 17; 26).

c. It is Yhwh's character and policy to be compassionate toward sinners who throw themselves on his mercy (25:6–7; 40:11–12; 41:4; 51:1–2; 86:5, 15; 130:3–4). So those whose trouble involves their sinfulness confess and acknowledge their wrongdoing and appeal to the mercy of the king for restitution.

3. The petitions and the way the prayers speak of divine response and intervention are at home in the military, political, and legal world of kingship.

a. The basic petition of the prayers, the counterpart of the nuclear cry of praise "Hallelujah," is "Save, Yhwh" (*Hôšî'ah Yhwh* 12:1; 20:9). In the forms "Save me/us/my life/thy people" the cry for salvation recurs frequently in the prayers, translated also as "deliver, give help, give victory," and the like (3:7; 6:4; 7:2; 22:21; 28:9; 31:16; 54:1; 59:2; 60:11; 69:1; 71:2; 86:16; 106:47; 108:6, 12; 109:26; 118:25; 119:94; 146). "Save" is accompanied by and alternates with corresponding terms (deliver, rescue, keep, redeem; on "judge/vindicate," see below). It was the role of the king to "save" his people in military danger (2 Sam. 10:27; Hos. 13:10) following the leaders of premonarchical times who were called "savior" and "judges/rulers" (figures in the book of Judges). In their early history before they had a king, Israel learned to depend on Yhwh's saving action through the institution of holy war (Deut. 20:1–4; see 1 Sam. 4:3; 14:6, 23, 39; 17:41). The motif of Yhwh's saving intervention seems to have had its definitive place in the wars of the people. This explains why the vocabulary and imagery of warfare are used so extensively in the first-person-singular prayers. It is an extended use of traditional salvation language; it can be used to describe Yhwh's saving intervention from any trouble.

b. The petition "Arise, Yhwh" fits into this picture. It was the old cry addressed to the Ark as the symbol of Yhwh of Hosts as the ritual invocation of the divine warrior, the prayer to Yhwh to intervene in human affairs against his enemies (Num. 10:35; Judg. 18:9; Ps. 132:8). The prayer sought the appearance of Yhwh in devastating theophanies like the ones described in Psalm 18:7–15. It is not surprising to find this petition in the prayers of the people for help (9:19; 44:26; 74:22; 82:8). But it shows up also in first-person-singular prayers (3:7; 7:6; 10:12; 17:13) as another use of the extension of salvation language to the plight of a single person. The divine warrior king intervenes even for the individual.

c. Another of the pleas for saving help takes the form "judge/vindicate me" (7:8; 26:1; 35:24; 43:1; see also the imperative "contend" in 35:1; 43:1; 74:22; 119:154). These petitions use the language of legal process to appeal to God, who is a righteous judge (7:11; 50:6). In Israel's legal system the king was the chief human legal officer, responsible for justice in the land (Ps. 72:1–4, of the Davidic king). Those in special trouble could appeal to the king's decision. The helpless, if they could reach the king with their cry "Save, O King," had a claim on his hearing their case (2 Sam. 14:4; 2 Kings 6:26). The prayers that use this language are cries to the divine King of Israel and all the earth to take their cause and vindicate their innocence in the matter at hand.

The theological setting-in-life in which all the prayers for help can be read is the relation of an *'ebed* to an *'adon*. It is more important in accounting for their formation and use than particular personal situations and cultic institutions. This setting incorporates all the various resources of experience and tradition used by their composers into one setting and intention—the speech of servants to their God and King about the troubles of life. It furnishes the common identity that goes with the use of the prayers. Along with the open, general character of their language, this setting evoked by the text of the songs is the feature that makes them useful and appropriate prayers through generations. To sing and pray and be led in reflection by these songs is to be set in the place where believers should and may bring the troubles of life. Wherever the major metaphor of the kingdom of God holds, the language, assumptions, and intentions of these songs are those of the right and useful prayers of the people of God.

— III —

The persons who pray in the prayers present themselves in terms of traditional categories. The prayers involve varying amounts of self-description. Their composers have used the various resources in the tradition of prayer language to create a kind of individuality in each psalm that must have had some relation to the person or kind of persons for whom it was composed. But this individuality appearing in a particular psalm is itself conformed to one or more types from a limited list.

The prayers use a number of terms to identify those whose petitions the prayers convey. There are two that are particularly important. In the self-description provided by the prayers, the person is either *'ani* or *ṣaddiq*, or both. These are the identities for whom the prayers were written and the ones for whom their use is appropriate. The terms can be translated by a range of English words. It is best to begin with the Hebrew, because the choice of any one translation may result in a reduction of the inclusiveness of the terms as they are used in the prayers.

*'Ani:* The term is used to designate those who pray (34:6; 40:17; 69:29; 86:1; 109:22). One of the prayers (Psalm 102) bears the title "A prayer of an *'ani*, when he is faint and pours out his plea before the LORD." The NRSV usually translates the term "poor," particularly when the word is paired with "needy," but also uses "afflicted" and "weak," and for the plural form adds "meek," "humble," "oppressed," "downtrodden." The New Jewish Publication Society Bible frequently renders it "lowly." In the psalms an *'ani* is one who is overwhelmed by troubles caused by the opposition and hostility of the strong and the wicked (10:2, 9; 14:6; 35:10; 37:14; 74:21; 109:16; plural 37:11; 147:6). The term is specific as to helplessness, indefinite as to the need. The *'ani* is in need not so much of something physical or economic as of help against powerful and wicked foes. The term is broadly inclusive and covers a variety of particular ills that render one unable to cope.

The prayers are founded on the belief that it belongs to the incomparable character of Yhwh to "deliver the lowly from those too strong for them" (35:10; 14:6; 34:6; plural 10:17; 25:9; 147:6; 149:4). It is important to remember that in these psalms it is not just a matter of the needy and their rights and hopes. The psalms are the prayers of those who in helplessness appeal to Yhwh, and by the very appeal say, "I am an *'ani,"* whether the term is used or not. The appeal of an *'ani* who is a servant of the LORD has a standing and a right with the divine King. Much of what is said in these prayers about the condition of the self, its relation to and trust in God, the power and wickedness of foes, is constitutive of an appeal by an *'ani* to the ultimate court of power in which his hope is placed.

In the course of the history of the practice and use of the prayers of the *'ani,* these beliefs about the relation of God to the lowly led toward thinking of *'ani* as the designation of a piety of trust and dependence. It referred to a religious attitude and stance as well as to particular circumstances. It came to mean a confession of neediness before God which belongs to the human condition. In some of the psalms there is a group who rejoice at the salvation of an *'ani* (22:26; 34:2; 69:32). They do not seem to represent any kind of institutionalized group, but rather those who self-consciously assume a faith of dependence, hope, and trust in God as against reliance on human resources.

So the poor and the suffering became instructors in the human condition. They gave the community the knowledge and the vocabulary to express the profound insight that before God and without God all are poor and afflicted, that mortality itself is a need of God. The poor and the suffering became types of a profound piety. This was not because there was any special virtue in poverty and affliction. Quite the contrary. Poverty and affliction were conditions that uncovered the need for God, the role in which one cried out for deliverance.

The prayers for salvation in the Psalter became the poetry of this theological type. They are liturgy for all, collectively and individually, from the least to the greatest, the weak and the strong, the poor and the prosperous, the sick and the healthy. They deny any the right to speak as independent, autonomous, invulnerable, strong. They disclose the ultimate identity of all with the needy and hurting. No one, they say, prays apart from his dependence and mortality. The risk of giving the language of poverty and suffering to every believer is, of course, great. It can lead to hypocrisy and trivialization. But the risk in not doing so is greater. The extension of the role of the lowly to all believers is the foundation for the Beatitudes: "Blessed are the poor in spirit . . . those who mourn . . . the meek . . . those who hunger and thirst for righteousness." It is the background of our LORD's instruction not to pray like the Pharisee who said, "God, I thank you that I am not like other men" (Luke 18:11).

*Ṣaddiq:* As you read the prayers, you come immediately upon the topic of righteousness (in Hebrew, the noun has a masculine and a feminine form, *ṣedeq and ṣedaqah;* the adjective frequently used as a substantive in singular and plural is *ṣaddiq).* Psalm 4 calls on "the God from whom my righteousness (*ṣedeq*) comes" (v. 1) and asserts "the LORD hears when I call" because "he has set apart the godly (*ḥasid*) for himself" (v. 3). Psalm 5 addresses the LORD as "a God who does not delight in wickedness" (v. 4) and prays "Lead me, LORD, in your righteousness (*ṣedaqah*)" (v. 8) in confidence that the LORD favors the righteous (*ṣaddiq*) with protection (v. 12). Psalm 7 lists a series of wrongs of which the one praying is innocent (vv. 3–4) and pleads that Yhwh judge the one praying according to his righteousness (*ṣedeq*, v. 8), in confidence that this righteous (*ṣaddiq*) God tests the minds and hearts in order to end the evil of the wicked and maintain the righteous (*ṣaddiq*, v. 10).

These prayers illustrate the way the topic figures in many of the psalms as a formative factor. In these songs the one who prays speaks of self as a *ṣaddiq*, whether the designation is actually used in the text or not. Human righteousness is related to divine righteousness, and both are set in polar opposition to human wickedness. This confident assumption of the status of the righteous in these psalms, and the separation of people into definite categories of the righteous and the wicked, is difficult and disturbing for those who pray the psalms today. These psalms can easily be reckoned expressions of self-righteousness and moralistic dogmatism, and have been. Their assumptions, intentions, and language need a particular effort to understand.

When the *ṣdq* words are used in the psalms, their meaning is somewhat different from the meaning we usually assign to righteousness, that is, character or conduct that meets the standards of what is just and moral. Rightness lies in the relation between a person's conduct and character and the standards in mind. For the *ṣdq* words the focus is not on absolute and self-contained norms, but on a community or social group and the pattern of relations of which it is composed. Rightness is a matter of the community's health and well-being (shalom), and of acts that create and foster its well-being. Righteousness is the character and condition of the community when things are in order for its shalom. Righteousness as conduct and activity is what benefits the community, makes things right. When things are bad, wrong, out of order, righteousness is salvific. Wickedness, the opposite of *ṣedaqah*, designates character and conduct that are adverse and destructive of the community and persons in it. It is in doing right by and in relationships that righteousness consists. And the variety of relationships of which life consists creates the variety in the specific substance of righteousness.

In the theological view of the psalms, righteousness belongs first of all to Yhwh. His blessing and ordering give rightness to Israel's life. When the people, and individuals among them, are in trouble, his intervention to set things right is his righteousness. Human righteousness is determined by the relation to God. The righteous are the congregation who respond in praise and joy. They are those who trust God and turn to him as their refuge in trouble. They are those who acknowledge him as true God and only God. Only those whose lives are ordered by the righteousness of God have a standing with him; they receive a renewal of righteousness in his blessing when they worship (Ps. 24).

Righteousness is defined also in the psalms in contrast to wickedness. Just as the strong enemy is the opposite of the lowly in the prayers, the wicked is the contrasting category to the righteous. The will and work of the wicked are destructive of the shalom God wills for his servants. They attack the relation to God and disturb the relation between people. In the theology of the psalms, there are only two possibilities for human beings in face of the reign of Yhwh. They may worship and live in the sphere of the divine righteousness or they may oppose it.

Generally, in the prayers in which righteousness is an issue, it is the case that the one who prays has had his relation to God and to others and so his own sense of himself called in question, attacked, and threatened. So when these psalms speak of the self to God, they present the self by using the features that go with the type of the *ṣaddiq* and disavow those which belong to the wicked. The psalmists believed it was possible to be faithful to Yhwh in worship and work. The prayers are the words of those who have undertaken to be faithful and then find their faithfulness put in doubt in one way or another. But no one in the psalms actually calls himself *ṣaddiq* before God. He says to God, "I am lowly and needy," but never "I am righteous." That is a determination that comes only from the divine side.

The considerations imply several points to be kept in mind in studying and interpreting the psalms in which the self is presented to God in contrast to the wicked.

1. These psalms are a witness to the immense importance of the topic of righteousness in every part of the Old Testament and in the New Testament. In scripture the righteousness of God and the righteousness of human beings are basic to faith, life, and theology. This is not a subject in which our contemporary piety and theology are very strong.

2. These psalms, like the others, work with typical language. They are not composed so as to reflect autobiographical preciseness and discrimination. The purpose of the self-description is to provide the one who prays with appropriate language in which to appeal to God. It is the formulaic language of the faithful, who believe and hope they may receive righteousness from their God, who tests and knows the heart. The distinction between the righteous and the wicked is like that in the Sermon on the Mount between those who are blessed and those who are not.

3. These are not prayers of self-righteousness; they are the prayers of those who need and hope for the justification of God. Nor are they utterances of legalistic righteousness. Even where the instruction (law) and statutes and ordinances come to the fore in the psalms, the emphasis is on the relation to God. The "law" is important because it is God's law and represents the way of the LORD.

4. These are not the prayers of those who are claiming perfection or sinlessness. They are, rather, the prayers of those who undertake faithfulness in the midst of the actual conditions of life, and who have tried to follow the way of the LORD instead of the way of the wicked.

5. These psalms are the prayers of those whose relation to God and to the community in which they live has been put in doubt. In the thought-world of the Bible, that raises the question of their righteousness. The experience of being questioned about one's relation to God and to community is a constant of the life of faith, though the forms of the question change. Accusation, misunderstanding, hostility, self-doubt, the presence and power of evil are all recurrently real. Christians will not use these prayers apart from the knowledge of the justification given in Jesus Christ. But the appropriation of and renewal in that grace must accompany the course of life.

— IV —

The trouble in which the one who prays is caught is a dominant feature of the prayers. The trouble is an important part of the identity of the person speaking the prayer. It is the personal setting of the prayer, its human cause. A description of the trouble is offered as part of the prayer as a way to claim God's attention and action (e.g., 3:1–2; 6:2–3, 6–7; 11:1–2; 13:1–2).

The description of trouble in these prayers is vivid and urgent. It is composed in words and phrases that convey anxiety, danger, insistence, even protest and complaint. But when we ask just what the specific trouble is, a certain answer is hard to come by. The actual difficulty is clothed in formulaic language, images, and metaphors drawn from various areas of experience.

The descriptions seem to use language generated primarily in three areas of experience: physical suffering and affliction, social conflict and alienation, and warfare. The areas have to be designated by rather general and imprecise terms, because in Israel's life conditions and situations that would be distinguished as different in our culture appear to have been referred to by the same vocabulary.

Sickness, in its most inclusive sense of all kinds of physical and psychic maladies, was a principal cause for the composition of prayers and the generation of language describing trouble. Psalms 38, 41, and 88 are rather pure examples of psalmic language generated by sickness. As in all comparable societies, illness was a common and desperate experience in ancient Israel. There were no medical resources. One had simply to hope to survive. Death was always a possibility, and mortality was frequent in every extended family. Indeed, death was experienced as already present in suffering and loss of vitality. Sickness was not viewed as a clinical phenomenon to be diagnosed and treated. It was, rather, experienced as a physical, social, and religious tragedy and spoken of in that way. It seems clear that the vocabulary of physical affliction came to be used metaphorically for other kinds of distress.

Another kind of trouble that led to the use of prayers for help and that shaped the language in which they were composed was accusation and persecution. For illustrations, read Psalms 5, 17, 27, 109. In Israel, the social unit in which one lived was of incalculable importance. For each person the extended family, kinship group, and community made up the sphere of life. There was little personal distance of the kind to which we are accustomed; independence and individualism did not exist. Most of the business of life was conducted on the personal level. It was the kind of society in which conflict was highly possible and very serious. In every case of conflict the honor, integrity, and rightness of the parties was at stake. A person who was accused by kin or neighbors or townspeople was called in question within the social unit and before God. The social resources for dealing with conflict were modest. A case could be taken to the local legal assembly that met in the gates. But testimony and argument there would often be contradictory and ambiguous. Violence by the stronger parties was always near at hand.

Descriptions of trouble in first-person-singular prayers also draw on the tactics, experiences, and weapons of warfare. That would be expected in the prayers of the larger community. What these motifs imply about the origin and use of first-person-singular prayers is quite uncertain. For examples, see Psalms 3, 11, and 35. Weapons and images of attack are employed often in describing the threat of enemies. That the king as leader of the nation would find himself in danger of a military nature and would pray about such danger in a typical way is understandable. There is the distinct possibility that the experiences of warfare were so common that its stock of language came to be used for other kinds of distress.

Some of the prayers seem deliberately general and vague, so as to cover more than one kind of trouble. Some seem to employ the language of different areas of experience in a kind of montage. Taken together, the three areas span the dimensions of human existence that compose our vulnerable mortality—we live in bodies, societies, and nations. There is a paradigmatic correspondence between the language of trouble in the prayers and the general human condition. Because human beings are physical and psychic creatures set in a pattern of relations to family, neighbors, and associates who as a group are cast into a historical movement with other groups, the prayers in the psalms speak the language of human affliction. That is what has made the prayers so open and useful to people in different ages and cultures. The individual who speaks in the psalm is recognizable; the psalmist's prayer can become the prayer of many.

Of course, if we could see the persons praying these prayers, their condition and circumstances would furnish the missing clue. Their predicament would give concreteness to the general, unspecified descriptions, would inform the formulaic with a core of personal reality. But to realize that is to grasp something very important about the way these prayers are written. They need a person to complete their meaning. Person and prayer go together. The prayer gives the person language to hold his or her need up to God. And the person, in using the prayer, interprets its openness and completes the identification of the one whose trouble is described in it.

The prayers collected in the book of Psalms have by the fact of their inclusion been dissociated from the actual circumstances for which they were originally written and from the rituals that would have accompanied their use. They are there to be studied as scripture and to be used in the ways that their openness and theology make possible.

— V —

Enemies are a frequent feature of the trouble described in the first-person-singular prayers. They are there as part of the trauma of suffering—hostile, accusing, expecting and wishing the worst for the one who prays. Whatever form trouble takes, the enemies are there in the situation of the psalmist. They are persons around the one who suffers, about whom he knows. But they are never specifically identified. The prayers do not tell *who* they are, only *what* they are. The enemies are part of the formulaic and typical character of these prayers. They are there because with the understanding of affliction and its prayers, which they represent, "enemies" play a *structural* and *necessary* role. Life-threatening trouble involves the experience of being beset by hostile forces. The enemies depicted in the prayers play this necessary interpretive role.

The images used to depict the enemies are the psalmist's distillation of a long tradition of such prayers and related genres. In the older prayers of a similar form from Mesopotamia, the hostile forces were demons, lesser gods, sorcerers, magicians with occult powers. The prayers were incantations of the power of one's personal god against these forces. In Israel, with its view of God and world, the assumptions about the nature and the meaning of physical and social affliction changed radically. All was understood in terms of the one God and human beings. But the formal literary traditions of portraying the hostile forces persisted.

The depictions of the enemies in the psalms draw on three traditional sets of metaphors: (1) Warfare: The enemies are portrayed as a hostile army at war against the afflicted (e.g., 3:11, 6; 27:3; 55:18). (2) Hunting and fishing: Enemies are portrayed as hunters and fishers, who pursue their quarry with all their instruments and skills (e.g., 7:15; 9:15; 31:4; 35:7–8). (3) Beasts: Enemies are portrayed as lions, dogs, wild oxen, and such (e.g., 7:2; 22:12–13, 20–21;

35:17). It is these images which give the enemies their uncanny and dramatic character, rendering them larger than life. This is not to say that, for the Israelites who used these prayers, there were no actual accusers or neighbors who made the worst of their afflictions, or persons who were in conflict with them. But the purpose of the portrayal of the enemy is to transcend the personal and the particulars of an individual's situation, in order to evoke its existential and religious dimensions.

In these prayers affliction is understood in terms of a world of personal forces. It is not diagnosed in a clinical way or rationalized in terms of any psychological or sociological theories or explained in terms of cultural peculiarities. It is experienced as the result of the will and actions of persons: others, self, and God. The normal and appropriate condition of life is constituted by wholeness and well-being (shalom) and by a rightness of conduct and character, in the fabric of relations in which life is set (*sedaqah*). The enemies are out to deprive the afflicted of either shalom or *sedaqah* or both. They attack life and the relation to God. That is what makes them theologically important and what makes them a symbol that can be used in other and quite different social and cultural settings from the one in which they were written. And it is this ultimate theological role of the enemies that accounts for the vehement prayers against them, the imprecations that seek their ruin. The imprecations are not based on personal hatred and vengefulness. They express, rather, the deep anxieties of the helpless in the face of powers that deprive them of life itself. They are fervent ways of saying that there are forces intervening between God and the one who prays which God alone can defeat. The prayers look to God for help, and the antagonists represent the alternative. This other possibility says, if the enemy prevails, then wills and minds other than God's would take on greater reality than God for the one who prays.

We pray because we desire that God's will and mind prevail in our lives—not our own, not others'. The role of the antagonists in the prayers represents, symbolizes, articulates the fact that prayer is made "in the presence of my enemies." The "world," in the Johannine sense, has all kinds of ways to put trust in question, to say to our finitude, "There is no help for you in God," to accuse and excite our sense of guilt.

It is instructive to note how the themes of the enemy to faith persist in Christian hymnody. Even a cursory survey of hymns written and sung across the ages turns up illustrations of their continuing structural role in the language of devotion: "Christian, dost thou see them, on the holy ground; how the powers of darkness rage thy steps around?" (fourth century). "Though Satan's wrath beset our path, and worldly scorn assail us, while Thou art near we will not fear; Thy strength will never fail us" (sixteenth century). "The soul that on Jesus hath leaned for repose, I will not, I will not desert to its foes" (eighteenth century). "Lo, the hosts of evil round us scorn Thy Christ, assail his ways. From the fears that long have bound us, free our hearts to faith and praise" (twentieth century).

It is the imprecatory psalms that set the severest problems for liturgy and theology. They are always mentioned in introductions as one of the problems of the psalms. Here are some matters to consider in dealing with this feature.

1. Prayer against the enemies, petitions that the enemies fail, be defeated, fall into their own traps, and so on, are features of many prayers for help (e.g., 5:10; 7:6, 9; 17:13–14; 28:4; 31:17–18; 35:4–6). The formulation of this element as extended imprecations or curses is simply on the upper end of the scale of intensity across which these petitions range (see 58:6–9; 69:22–28; 83:9–18; 109:6–19; 140:9–11).

2. The interpreter can distinguish between the use of these prayers as liturgy and as scripture, though the two are, of course, related.

3. Jesus (Matt. 5:43–48; Luke 9:51–56) and Paul (Rom. 12:14–21) instruct Christians to love, bless, and pray for their enemies. That instruction forbids prayer against our human enemies.[1] The use of the imprecations in liturgy in any plain or literal sense is rejected. We remember, however, that the early church established a tradition of opposing sin, death, and the devil with such psalms.

4. The psalms reflect an understanding of salvation that takes place in this world and this life. As composed in Old Testament times, they anticipated no eschatological compensation or vindication. The situation assumed by these prayers is that of an either-or. Where there are relentless foes of the oppressed or accused, one will be vindicated and the other defeated or condemned. Prayers against the foes are a form of plea for God's help.

5. The prayers against enemies are not unique in their understanding of God's action against the oppressor, the arrogant, the wicked, and such. The intervention of God that is sought is quite the same as called for by the law (compare Ps. 109:9 and Ex. 22:23) and the prophets (see the announcements of judgment).

6. The enemies are not depicted in the prayers as merely personal or political adversaries. They characteristically put the trust or integrity of the one who prays in question, do not pay attention to the way of God, challenge the justice and loyal love of God. They attack the religious dimension of existence. It is this feature of the psalmic enemy that led Luther to distinguish between issues of love and faith and to say, "Love does not curse or take vengeance, but faith does,"[2] and led Calvin to caution that prayers against others are to be prayed only under the guidance of the Holy Spirit, free of all self-interest, passion, and foolishness.[3] Note the anathemas of Paul in 1 Cor. 16:22; 1 Tim. 1:20.

7. These prayers have often been assessed as ways of leaving vengeance to

God, as his decision, rather than taking violent action (Rom. 12:19). They are a way to turn to prayer rather than to revenge (Pss. 109:4; 69:12–13).[4]

— VI —

In spite of challenges that the interpretation and use of the prayers in the Psalter involve, the effort required to understand and appropriate them will be richly rewarded. These prayers may be theologically the most intense texts in the Bible. In their language is the confession of a neediness that underlies the needs of mortality and failure, of finitude and fallibility. What these prayers really seek in all their pleading is God, that God should become "my salvation," that God should be "my God." Psalm 63:1, 3 discloses the impulse that informs them all:

> O God, you are my God, I seek you,
> my soul thirsts for you;
> my flesh faints for you,
> as in a dry and weary land where there is no water. . . .
> Because your steadfast love is better than life,
> my lips will praise you.

# CHAPTER 4

# MEANS OF GRACE
## The Benefits of Psalmic Prayer

"Means of grace" is a term used recurrently in the Christian tradition for regular and established ways in which divine grace is offered and received. The list of means has usually included the sacraments, reading scripture, and prayer. The psalms composed as prayers of need, gratitude, and trust have provided one of the most important resources in the disciplined use of means of grace. The prayer psalms are both scripture and prayer. Everything that we know about their role in the life of faith across the centuries is a record of their significant value.

This chapter seeks to identify and describe some of the ways in which the prayer psalms have served and can serve the practice of prayer. Awareness of their proven and potential benefits is useful in the work of interpretation and in the appropriation of the prayer psalms as our personal and corporate prayer. Through the ages the prayer psalms have been a gift of prayer, instruction in prayer, and encouragement to pray.

### A Gift of Prayer: What to Pray

1. These songs form "a chain of prayer" across the ages. In the matter of prayer they are, along with the Lord's Prayer, our primary tradition. The open and symbolic character of their language makes them accessible and meaningful to people in different eras and cultures. Their agenda matches the continuities of the human condition under God. The chain reaches from David through Jeremiah and Jesus and Paul and the church fathers and the monks and Reformers to us. Availing themselves of these psalms, all have prayed and learned to pray. In using these prayers we join ourselves to that great company, and our own practice and understanding of prayer is encouraged and challenged by the use they have made of these prayers and the spiritual fruit that use bore in their lives.

2. These prayers give us words to say. When we need to pray, we are not

always ready with words. Words are important in prayer. It must be spoken. Impulses and feelings, reflections and musings, anxieties and hopes that remain inarticulate are, in the view of the psalms, not yet prayer. By these psalms we are led in prayer. There is a phrase, recurrent in these prayers, that says, literally translated, "I cry to you with my voice" (*qara'ti beqoli*). The phrase is one psalmic hint that prayer, even in private devotions, is most actual when said aloud. To speak aloud to God is to cross the threshold from thought to direct address. It is the way to actualize the trust that God is there, present for our praying, hearing our prayers.

3. The prayer psalm can, when said, evoke the setting in which prayer occurs. The utterance calls forth what the Bible calls a *maqom*, a special place where God is present for the human being. God's name is called, the name that is his presence and bears all the qualities of his person. To "call on the name of God" is to place oneself in his presence. The prayer describes the self, presents the self to God in all its weakness and need. It lets the self be in the real Presence. Through the psalm the self speaks to God. All that is essential to the place of prayer is brought about with the saying of the psalm.

## Instruction in Prayer: How to Pray

1. These prayers locate our praying in the reign of God. Because they are the prayers of servants to their king and God, they seek in one way or another the kingdom of God. There is an ancient tradition among their interpreters that these prayers expound the Lord's Prayer. The tradition holds that when the disciples asked Jesus to teach them to pray, he said, Pray *like this*, and gave them in his prayer an outline or agenda that may be filled out with psalmic prayer. In every age interpreters have used the phrases of the Lord's Prayer as rubrics to order and signify elements of the psalms. It is amazing what perspectives are opened up by this discipline. Take "Our Father who art in heaven," and see how many ways the prayer psalms portray "God above us." Take "Hallowed be thy name," and pay attention to the great significance of the name of the LORD in these prayers. Or, especially, take "Thy kingdom come" and search out the ways in which these prayers seek the kingdom of God and its righteousness.

2. These psalms place prayer in its right context, alongside and paired with praise of God. In the context of the book of Psalms, they are mingled with hymns of praise. In the context of their structure, they typically include elements of praise. By the Hebrew title of the book (*tehillim*—praises) they are classified in their canonical identity as texts for the praise of God. The prayers of a person in trouble anticipate and are consummated in a song of praise for the salvation the LORD has given. Even the most desperate pleading, demanding prayer is ruled nonetheless to be praise of God. By this constant correlation with praise, prayer at its extreme limits is held to a

centering and founding in God, rather than self. It is a witness to God and does not descend into testimony that has self as subject.

3. The prayer psalms locate the center and identify the essence of prayer in petition. The prayers for help are organized around a petition; songs of thanksgiving celebrate a petition answered; the psalms of trust testify to a life based on help received and anticipated. As a group, they point to petition as the pivot on which real prayer turns. Not to ask is to fail to recognize in prayer who God is and who we are.

Correspondingly, the prayers for help give those who use them their rightful roles: petitioners. They teach us to say, "I am poor and needy." They invite us to shed our postures of autonomy, pride, competence in the ultimate issues of life, defensiveness. "Before God we are all beggars" (Martin Luther).

4. The prayers in their three modes express a structural pattern of religious experience: need, gratitude, and trust. The prayers for help, the songs of praise for help, and the songs of trust reflect a movement from helplessness through salvation to gratitude and to the life of trust based on the experience of salvation. According to the Old Testament story, the movement happened *for the people* of God, particularly in the exodus and exile, *and for individuals*. The movement is the basic pattern of the Christian's relation to God through Christ. We are helpless before sin and death, delivered by God's salvific work in Christ to gratitude and joy, for a life of trust based on that salvation. The movement happens to us once in a foundational way. It is repeated, in a renewing rhythm, as we recurrently receive and reclaim the benefits of Christ as we move through the vicissitudes of life. The foundational experience lies behind, secures, and informs the subsequent ones. But we continue through our lives to need the help of God, to praise God for the gift of grace, and to live in a trust based on God's salvation. Our foundational experience of salvation and its reflection in the course of our lives is the hermeneutical context in which all three forms of the songs of trouble become the language of our life.

## Encouragement to Prayer: Why We Pray

1. The prayers for help encourage us *to speak of the worst* of life to God, and they teach us to do it in language that is adequate to and honest about feelings of suffering, anxiety, alienation. These prayers witness that God is concerned, involved, responsive to, and even responsible for his servants in their affliction.

2. The prayers for help *give human finitude a place* alongside human fallibility in the way we present ourselves to God in public as well as private prayer. They instruct us to pray about the troubles of our mortality as well as the failings of our sinfulness. We are accustomed in liturgy to present

ourselves to God first through the confession of sin, and so to emphasize penitence as the one necessary thing in our relation to God. The prayers uncover the ways in which the troubles of mortality affect our relation to God, and they pose the question of why this disorientation should not be confessed. Many of the prayers deal only with finitude, and some only with fallibility, while some mingle the two. As a text, they pose the question about the relation between the two in God's way with human beings and in the course of our own lives.

3. The prayers for help are a *theological interpretation of suffering*. They place the troubles of life in a context of meaning. They provide the way to move affliction out of the realm of merely accidental, fortuitous meaninglessness into the comprehension of a view of self, world, and God. Suffering, when it hurts enough and threatens the self enough, wrenches out a "Why?" and a "Why me?" even for those who do not believe there is a God to answer. In this way, the need to make some sense of our existence as part of our very being is structural to human nature. It is there in the human, even if it takes only the negative form of despair, bitterness, resignation. For the radical monotheist, suffering must be experienced in faith in God. These prayers are language with which faith speaks of suffering. Therefore it is inappropriate to use words like "despair" in describing their mood and stance. God, even when spoken of as distant, is addressed.

The threefold pattern used in the prayers to describe trouble is a comprehensive pattern of the nature and experience of affliction. The descriptions typically speak of trouble afflicting the one who prays in terms of self, other, and God, or in the direct address of the prayers, as I, they, you.

a. This threefold pattern is rooted in Israel's understanding of the kinds of affliction that generated the language used to describe trouble in these songs. Sickness, accusation, and conflict all had clearly defined social and religious as well as personal dimensions. This pattern corresponds to the general experience that trouble that puts the existence and/or status of the self in question is never experienced as merely personal. It evokes the social and theological dimensions of existence. It affects one's view of and relation to others and theirs to you. It brings to consciousness the finitude and dependence, the fallibility and accountability, that are structures of every life. The threefold pattern in the songs has a paradigmatic and symbolic capacity to mirror and express the sufferings of individuals and social groups. This capacity is one of the features of these songs that make them so open to all kinds of conditions and so useful to people in different eras and cultures.

b. This paradigmatic and symbolic character has also made these prayers open to a general use. They have been related not only to specific situations and cases of suffering, but to neediness of the human condition. The trouble described in these prayers is always one in which life and its relation to God are in one way or another at stake. At the least, those who pray have been put in dependence on God. At worst, they may have provoked the wrath of God. The enemies are not merely their personal enemies. The stance and action of these "workers of evil" are hostile to God and to God's servant. They serve death and alienation. Because of these features the prayers can be read and said as the voice of the human predicament. The life of faith is not spared the troubles of mortality and failure, and continues in a world where forces hostile to the beliefs and hopes and ways of faith have power. We want to live, and we are dying. We want to be in control of our lives, but life happens to us. We want to be with others, but we are unknown and, in our hearts, alone. We need the justification of our existence, but we are questioned, ignored, condemned. In all these matters our relation to God is at stake, and they can be borne and resolved only in the salvation of God.

4. The prayers for help are *action taken against suffering.*

a. *At the psychological level* the description of suffering in prayers moves physical and mortal pain from the sensory and psychological spheres to that of language. In doing so, they bring what is felt into reach of the distinctively human dimension where will and thought, memory and anticipation, can get at it. This allows us to realize that we are more than the experience of pain, that there is a self that can put it apart, at even a little distance, view it, and speak about it.

b. *At the social level* the description of trouble moves the pain from isolation to company. Self-description conveys what is felt to others who can hear, sympathize, and share in empathy. When used with a pastor or a circle of fellow believers, the wall of loneliness is broken. It always helps to tell someone. When another knows, the power of suffering is diminished a bit.

c. *At the theological level* the description of trouble moves the pain from the human sphere, with its possibilities, to the sphere of divine possibilities of meaning and help. God is told. The prayer is made in certainty that God hears, and simply to be heard by God is help. The prayers are based, moreover, on the belief that the final and full will of the LORD does not purpose suffering. Even in the prayers where suffering is taken to be the work of God's wrath, appeal is made to God's loving-kindness and compassion.

There are kinds and cases of suffering in one's own life and in the lives of others about which the servants of the LORD can and should take action. The law and the prophets so instruct us. But prayer should accompany the effort, lest we think and act as though deliverance could be our business alone. There are kinds and cases of trouble against which prayer is the only action we can take.

5. The prayers are *appeals for salvation.* All the songs of trouble turn on the subject of salvation. The prayers call on the "Savior of those who seek refuge" (Ps. 17:7). All the songs are based on the knowledge that "salvation belongs to the LORD" (3:8). The words associated with "save/salvation" are woven through their texts. The petitions never seek mere things. Nor do they

concern trivial or routine problems. Because the situation is always one that is life-threatening to the physical and/or social existence of the self, the prayers are in one way or another prayers for the salvation of life. The situation is always one that raises a question about the relation to God. So in their ultimate intention the prayers seek God—not just relief from the specific trouble, or justification in the face of accusing questions, but God in and through the relief and justification. They are the voice of longing for God. They reach out for the change that will make one able to say, "You have become my salvation" (118:21).

# CHAPTER 5

# A QUESTION OF IDENTITY
## The Threefold Hermeneutics of Psalmody

In his *Confessions* Augustine tells how he used the psalms as his own prayer: "What utterances I used to send up unto Thee in those Psalms, and how was I inflamed toward Thee by them" (IX, 4). Athanasius said of the psalms: "They seem to me to be a kind of mirror for everyone who sings them in which he may observe the motions of the soul, and as he observes them give utterance to them in words" *(Epistle to Marcellinus on the Interpretation of the Psalms)*. He was seconded by Calvin, who wrote in the introduction to his commentary: "I am wont to call them an anatomy of all parts of the soul; for no-one will find in himself a single feeling of which the image is not reflected in the mirror."[1]

Historical comment on the psalms is strewn with such observations. These remarks testify to a general and continuous experience. Christians found themselves and came to expression in the language of the psalms. Their own self was identified with, and identified by, the self whose voice speaks in these prayers.

When Christians talked like that, they were referring especially to one group of psalms, the prayers and songs composed as the voice of an individual. It was these psalms, in the first person, that invited an awareness of self and offered language to self. There are far more of them in the book of Psalms than hymns of praise and poetry of instruction. By the weight of their number they dominate the Psalter and give a cast and tone to the whole.

Psalm 13 illustrates their character quite well. The psalm is brief. In spite of its brevity it contains all the features that are typical of these prayers. Hermann Gunkel called it a "parade example" of the type.

> How long, O Lord, will you continue to forget me?
> How long will you hide your face from me?
> How long must I bear pain in my soul,
>     sorrow in my heart all day long? . . .

Listen, answer me, O LORD my God!
Lighten my eyes, lest I sleep in death,
     lest my enemy say, "I have prevailed,"
     lest my foes rejoice because I am shaken.
I trust in your steadfast love
     my heart shall rejoice in your salvation.
I will sing to the LORD
     because he has helped me.

The majority of the first-person psalms are such prayers. They are the appeal of a person in trouble. There are some fifty of them in the book. There is real variety in the group in length, arrangement, and content, but they are held together as a group in two important ways. First, they are consistently composed of a common set of elements. They name God and speak in direct address to the LORD. They feature descriptions of trouble that is personal or social or theological, in various combinations. Each is organized around a petition for the person to be heard and helped. Trust is avowed. A promise of praise and sacrifice that will testify to the sought deliverance is made.

The second common characteristic of these prayers is what may be called paradigmatic openness. Those who speak in the psalms describe themselves and their situation, but they do it in a way that draws a verbal portrait of a set of types, rather than of a specific person. The language of description is formulaic and metaphoric. It creates types of persons and predicaments. The descriptions offer roles that suit the continuing structures of neediness in human experience. It is precisely this commonality and this openness which have rendered this group of psalms so available for the uses of corporate liturgy and private devotion. For nearly two millennia, Christians have sung, chanted, and murmured these psalms as their prayers. In acts of worship and devotion they spoke of God and self and world with the words the psalms provided. They found and knew themselves through these prayers.

It is, however, a fact that these prayers have become difficult and strange for contemporary Christians. Where our predecessors in prayers received and used this language with a sense of recognition, discovery, and illumination, it has become problematic for many in our time. We hear these prayers of pain and anguish as coming from another quarter: this voice that speaks so insistently, pleads and protests and even argues; this voice that addresses an absent God directly, as if God were there, a presence; this soul riven by a desperate dependence for rightness and life; this pilgrim who must make a way, as if through a dark valley surrounded by foes, to trust and obedience; this human whose desire will not be satisfied by anything less than the experience of God. This individual in the prayer psalms has come to be different, a stranger, sometimes embarrassing.

The public evidence for this sense of discontinuity with the tradition of psalmody began to appear, I think, in the movement away from a complete Psalter in communions that had always used one. Where selections of psalms for singing and reading were made, it was psalms of this particular group that were omitted. Those that were included were frequently edited to omit portions felt to be difficult. The first version of the contemporary Common Lectionary was sparse in its use of the prayers for help. Emphasis on worship as celebration made them sound incongruent in liturgy. Understandings and fashions of prayer that do not easily accommodate the standpoint and mood of psalmic prayers are widespread. The prayer psalms visibly lost their place as the canonical core of corporate liturgy and private devotion.

What brought about the rupture between the self evoked in the psalm and the self-awareness of believers? The problem is more than simple historical and cultural distance. After all, the correlation had lasted nearly two thousand years. What are the reasons? A liberal optimism about the human condition? A stolid, technical literalism that lost the feel for the poetic, metaphorical, and mythic as mediums of reality? Theologies that obscured the face of a God who could (or would) answer the cry, "Hear me, help me"? Surely there are various related reasons, sometimes gathered up under the sign of modernity.

There is currently a revival of interest in this sector of psalmody. In part the interest has been stimulated by the liturgical renewal, with its concern to restore the psalms to their traditional role in the repertoire of worship. The latest version of the Common Lectionary uses 112 psalms, of which thirty-two are prayer psalms. After decades of omission, Presbyterians again have a hymnal that includes a Psalter. It offers seventy-six psalms, twelve of them prayers for help.

In part, the interest expresses the realization of pastors and those in pastoral care disciplines that these psalmic prayers give people language to express the distresses that press against the limits of our customary banal, trivial, deceptive talk. Range, frustration, depression, grief, failure all can find a voice here not available in the usual confines of liturgy or the normal circumspection of pastoral engagement. These are positive and promising moves toward the recovery of psalmic prayer.

And yet one must entertain serious doubt whether these moves get at the central alienation between people and psalms. It probably will not work simply to put these prayer psalms back in the service. They will likely remain the utterance of some person unknown and not understood. It will not do to employ them simply as a resource of counseling and therapy, a tool of catharsis that uses them to express a self-consciousness that is already there. The authentic use of the psalmic prayers in the tradition has involved, not just the expression of the self through the psalms, but as well, and most important of all, *a self-realization* that comes with *using* these prayers.

— II —

What was the nature of the transaction between these psalms and those who prayed them? With that question on my mind, I came upon a comment in the Midrash *Tehillim* on Psalm 18: "R. Yudan taught in the name of R. Judah: all that David said in his Book of Psalms applies to Himself, to all Israel and to all the ages." That is, the identity offered by the Psalm is not simple but complex, not singular but threefold. Whoever prays Psalm 18, said these rabbis, assumes a self constituted of a relation to David and to the people of God and to mortal humanity.

One recognizes the parallel to early Christian interpretation. Augustine on Psalm 3 provides a typical illustration. Here are some phrases culled from his discussion about who speaks in the prayer: "Christ speaks to God in his human nature . . . ; both the Church and her head . . . cry out with the lips of the prophet . . . ; which of the faithful cannot make this language their own?" Again, the consciousness of a threefold identity. The individual in the psalm is constituted of an interrelation between Christ, church, and the Christian.

It would be easy to dismiss this transaction as a hermeneutical artifact, the practice of allegory or typology. I do not, however, think it is fair to the matter to assess this understanding as merely the result of a theory of reading applied in a somewhat technical way. It is, rather, an account of what happened when the psalms were used as scripture and liturgy—that is, when in the synagogue the prayers of David were read as liturgy of the congregation and meditation of the pious; and when in the church the psalms were read under the direction of their use by Christ in the Passion as the liturgy of worship and the prayers of believers. Hermeneutical theory, to the degree that was important, was generated by practice rather than the other way around.

It may be important for our history-oriented mentality and its concern about original meaning to bring yet another matter into consideration. This approach did not originate in the synagogues and churches of the first centuries of our era. It is a continuation of what happened in making the book of Psalms. The process by which the book was formed and the resulting canonical shape of the book argue that the psalms as we have them are the voice of a composite identity rather than the voice of some specific historical individual. The psalms in which an individual speaks have "an original meaning" only in a complex, multivalent sense. In their very composition they are crafted of poetic idioms and typical features that together create a persona intentionally open to use by different and successive persons. The prayers and the prayer types originally designed for use by individuals in time came to be the vehicle for the community. The congregation came to understand itself and to pray in a common solidarity as an I as well as a we. The individual prayers were used as corporate liturgy. In time the story of

David became the context, first for the individual prayers, and then for many of the psalms. In the very making and shape of the book, the psalm prayers are understood and used as the voice of the messiah, the people of God, and the faithful individual. The synagogue and early church did not violate the psalms in reading them in three interrelated ways. They continued the hermeneutical understanding and experience that created the book of Psalms.

As I have thought about this testimony of the rabbis and Augustine, it has begun to dawn on me what is at issue here: a way of prayer far profounder than the one I practice, one learned because the communities of faith prayed these psalms in an awareness of the three selves of which their identity was constituted.

A way of prayer that is *christological, not just autobiographical,*
a reading of these psalms as words that witness to the identification of Christ with our humanity.
A way of prayer that is *corporate, not just individual,*
a use of these first-person psalms as the voice of the community and of others in it in vicarious representative supplication.
A way of prayer that is *typical, rather than subjective,*
a saying of these psalms to create a consciousness of who and what we are, rather than as expressions of a consciousness already there.

I want to reflect on each of these ways of construing the first-person prayers in the psalms *in the form of questions*—questions because this threefold hermeneutics of prayer involves habits of consciousness that are difficult to acquire in our time.

— III —

The first question: Can we, should we, find in these prayers of dereliction and trust an evocation of the passion of our Lord?

I am not proposing that we understand them as prophecy, in the specific sense that term has in the classification of literature. These psalms were not composed aforetime to predict events and experiences of suffering that would come true in the life of Jesus. There is a nod toward this approach in the New Testament (see John 19:28). There is a long and important tradition of reading psalms as prophecy in the history of Jewish and Christian interpretation, but that approach is not underwritten by what has been learned about the character and purpose of the psalmic prayers.

They are, rather, the literary deposit in the scriptures that testifies to the range and depth of anguish that can and does come to those who are mortal and vulnerable and undertake to live unto God. They are the classics of life that undergoes the worst *in* faith and *for* the faith. They are the paradigms of the soul that uses affliction, alienation, pain, and even dying as occasions to assert the reality and faithfulness of God. As such they can show us in detail the mortality that belongs to Christ in his identity with us.

The Gospels draw on the psalms more than on any other sector of the Old Testament to tell the story of Jesus. Particularly, the narrative of the passion of Jesus uses language and motifs from them extensively. Features from Psalms 22 and 31 and 69 appear recurrently in the narrative. These psalms are not used as prediction and fulfillment, but as elements of the story itself. The self-description of those who pray in the psalms becomes a scenario that Jesus enacts. He identifies himself with and through them, assumes their affliction, speaks their language.

The way that the Gospels use the psalmic prayers to tell the story of Jesus, the way that Jesus enters into the identity of the voice and experience heard in the psalms, must mean that these prayers are intended as a major commentary on the meaning of his affliction. The relationship advises that the sufferings of Jesus were not unique. Their significance does not lie in the amount or measure, but in the typicality. The identification of Jesus with the self who speaks in the psalms is the sign of the representative and corporate reality of his passion. He suffers and prays with all those whose suffering and praying is represented by such prayers. He enters into their predicament. The hurt and cry of that great choir of pain is gathered into his life and voice. Henceforth the voice of affliction in these psalms is inseparable from the voice of Jesus. They are the liturgy of his incarnation, the language of his assumption of our predicament.

He is one of us and one with us in our mortal humanity. Yet, can we rely on our own experience, our self-consciousness, our language to grasp what his passion, his identification with the human predicament involves? We are too petty in our complaints, too limited in our empathies, too inhibited in our language. We will usually trivialize, but these psalmic prayers for help do not trivialize. Indeed, they seem one vast exaggeration until read looking toward his life. When we ask with Gerhardt's great hymn on the Passion, "What language shall I borrow to thank thee, dearest friend, for this thy dying sorrow?" can there be any other answer?

Can we learn to say these prayers as a way of hearing Christ pray in and for our humanity? Can we say them as the voice of his unending passion in and for our mortality?

— IV —

The second question: Could the problem of our relation to the persons praying in these psalms lead us to a different understanding of how we use the first-person pronoun when we pray, the meaning with which we say "I/me/my"?

The use of the first-person psalms in Christian liturgy and devotion is complicated by a difference between Israel and contemporary Christians in consciousness of self and social group. The first-person pronoun had a different content and structure then. The individual Israelite received identity and significance from identity with the group. To say "I" meant to speak of one's group as well as one's person. We bring our identity to a group, differentiate ourselves within it, join it, accept its ways and opinions, expect the group to nurture the individual and to justify itself to the individual.

In Israel, there was a real corporate identity, which could say "I" authentically. And the individual said "I" in congruence with and not in distinction from the group. So the use of the first-person psalms by individuals today will work differently. We contextualize them in our identities. We wonder at the disparity between our experience and the experience described in the psalms because we don't think of ourselves typically or corporately.

Can we learn to say these prayers in liturgy and in devotion as an act of empathy and sympathy, as an expression of solidarity with others? Could we give voice to their pain and need, make these supplications serve as intercessions for them as one with us, as the body of Christ, as the totality of humanity?

The psalmic prayers come to us from the history of their use with the "I" already expanded to "we." It helps us to use our imagination and remember how many countless thousands in all the ages have left their marks on these prayers: Jeremiah and Jesus and Paul and Augustine and Calvin and Wesley and the Highlanders of Scotland and the Huguenots—and you complete the list. Know that history, and you cannot say and sing them without hearing the echoing chorus of "all the saints who from their labors rest, who thee by faith before the world confessed."

But, our corporateness is a fact not only of yesterday but of today.

Could the use of these prayers remind us and bind us to all those in the worldwide church who are suffering in faith and for the faith? All may be well in our place. There may be no trouble for the present that corresponds to the tribulations described in the psalms. But do we need to do more than call the roll of such places as El Salvador, South Africa, and Palestine to remember that there are sisters and brothers whose trials could be given voice in our recitation of the psalms? The old church believed that it was all the martyrs who prayed as they prayed the psalmic prayers.

Would it be possible to say them for the sake of and in the name of the fellow Christians known to us? We do make intercessions for them, but perhaps these psalms can help us do more than to simply, prayerfully wish grace and help for them, can help us to find words to represent their hurt, alienation, failure, and discouragement.

Then there is the whole world of humanity beyond the church known and unknown to us, who have neither the faith nor the language to hold their misery up before God. In the day-to-day course of events they may become simply part of the scenery of life, features in the newspaper or in the evening news. These prayers are so poignant and vivid that they give concreteness and personal actuality to what is happening beyond the range of our personal experience.

The apostle said "If one member suffers, all suffer together" (1 Cor. 12:26) and he also said, "Bear one another's burdens." Can these prayers become a way of doing that?

— V —

The third question: Could the problem of our relation to the person praying in the psalms lead us to a deeper, truer, more ultimate awareness of who and what we are, why, and that we need to pray for help?

The problem is certainly there. We live and think and feel as part of modern Western culture. It is true of that culture that it is not informed with the active consciousness of mortality that was characteristic of earlier ages, and which is still characteristic for much of the rest of the world. But these psalmic prayers give the clear impression that they were composed in a culture and out of a consciousness structured by a sense of life's vulnerability.

In recent years the Israelis have been conducting an archaeological excavation of a cemetery at a location near the walls of Jerusalem called Giv'at ha-Mivtar. The burials in the cemetery are dated to the second and first centuries B.C. As the archaeologists have cataloged and identified the remains in the cemetery, they have learned that about 60 percent of the people who were buried there had died before they reached the age of twenty-five. Only 6 percent were sixty years old or older. It doesn't take much imagination to grasp what that meant for the sense of life.

The change from that kind of situation is very recent. A few years ago a professor at the University of North Carolina published a book titled *Children of Pride*. It is composed of a collection of letters that he found and edited, letters that had been written between the members of a family who lived in the early 1800s just south of Savannah, Georgia. The letters are filled with the news of sickness and dying as part of the normal scene. The regular occurrence of illness and death creates such an ordinary part of the texture of life that it is difficult for a contemporary to imagine what it must have been like. As I read the book I remembered the dying of my grandfather, who in 1928 acquired an erysipelas infection for which there was no help. Nowadays, its healing is a fairly simple matter with antibiotics.

In our culture this situation has all changed dramatically, and for that we thank God. Now the old outnumber the young, and the problems we ponder are the problems of people being kept alive.

And yet, is it true if we say that we are not still essentially needy—that is, mortal, limited in our competence to manage what happens to us, vulnerable to events and to others—that we do not need divine help? In the long view, ultimately speaking, there is no technical or scientific solution to the reality of human finitude and sinfulness. To be human is to desire life and rightness, and because we cannot autonomously secure either, to be essentially needy.

Could we use these prayers to learn that, admit that, to learn from them to nurture a consciousness structured by an honest sense of our finitude and fallibility? The Jewish novelist Isaac Bashevis Singer once said, "I only pray when I am in trouble. But I am in trouble all the time."[2]

## — VI —

I must leave these questions with you. The answers for each of us and for the contemporary community of faith can be found only in the practice and experience of prayer. Can we discover through these psalm-prayers an identity that is christological, corporate, and typical? Can they break up and break into our preoccupying subjectivity and imperious individualism? Can their use bring us intimations of the consciousness the apostle spoke of when he wrote such sentences as: "Wretched man that I am! Who will rescue me from this body of death?" (Rom. 7:24); and "You are the body of Christ and individually members of it" (1 Cor. 14:27); and "It is no longer I who live, but it is Christ who lives in me" (Gal. 2:20)?

In 1990 Walker Percy died, and we lost one of the few Christian voices in contemporary literature. As the introduction to one of his books, to which he gave the whimsical title *Lost in the Cosmos: The Last Self-Help Book*, he used quotations from Nietzsche and Augustine. The first begins, "We are unknown, we knowers, to ourselves." The second runs, "O God, I pray you to let me know my self." Perhaps the answer to that prayer may be found also in our time in the prayers of the Psalter.

# CHAPTER 6

# HEAR ME, HELP ME
## An Interpretation of Psalm 13

"A cry means something only in a created universe. If there is no creator, what is the good of calling attention to yourself?" (E. M. Cioran). Psalm 13 is a cry at the center of which is a plea: "Notice me! Answer me!" (v. 3). The plea is addressed to the LORD, the creator of heaven and earth and of Israel. The psalm is language in which the desperate loneliness of human life is offered to God, who is its ultimate source and only final help. It is a prayer in which mortals in anxiety and anguish speak of themselves *to* God and in doing so speak *about* God to those of us who read the prayer as scripture.

Though it is the shortest of the prayers for salvation in the book of Psalms, it comprehends their essential elements so completely that to know it is to have an introduction to the others. Hermann Gunkel called it a "parade example" of its type. It belongs to the kind of prayer that has been named, somewhat misleadingly, the lament of an individual. The clear structure shows by its components and their order that it is ever so much more than a lament. It is composed in three parts: a description of trouble (v. 1–2), a petition for help (vv. 3–4), and praise of the LORD (vv. 5–6). The parts contain a sequence of components, each of which plays a role in the prayer as an act of faith.

The psalmist describes the experience of trouble out of which the prayer arises in terms of a relation to God (v. 1), of his own suffering (v. 2ab), and of his helplessness before an enemy (v. 2c). The three elements of the description make up the fundamental paradigm of a lament, which typically portrays a predicament in terms of you (God), I (the one who prays), and they (the social context of the trouble). Though the three are distinct, they are not separable. Their interrelation can be understood by beginning with the third or with the first. We might reason that the enemy's threat is the cause of the anxiety and anguish felt by the psalmist, who regards both as signs of the absence of God. The prayer moves the other way, beginning theologically: God's absence is the source of the psalmist's anxious wondering in the face of the enemy's threat. The reality of God is such a crucial environment of his life that the psalmist cannot think or feel without thinking and feeling in terms of God's relation to him. What the precise trouble is, the text does not say. We deal with prayer, not autobiography. Here one speaks to God as to a friend who already knows all the details that our words assume. We hear only of an enemy whose hostility is a threat to life, of foes who would find pleasure in the psalmist's undoing.

The petition is twofold: a plea to be heard (v. 3a) and a plea for help (v. 3b). This twofold petition is also typical of such psalms, but the distinction between God's hearing and his helping is more formal than real. Any word that faith can take as an answer from God is help that breaks the loneliness of isolation and brings vitality to a waning hold on life. And any help for helplessness may be read by faith as an answering word. Two motive-clauses support the petition: "lest I sleep in death . . . lest my enemy say . . . " The psalmist dares to believe that his life and his weakness matter to God. The basis of that confidence is hidden in the vocative "my God." The LORD has bestowed on the one who prays as a member of the elect community an identification with himself, a reason and right to say "my God" in anticipation and hope. More than any other resource of language, the little pronoun "my" reaches out to another person to disclose and claim an identification of self in terms of the other. When one says "my God" in prayer, it is a recognition that the possibility of life in the fullest sense of that word rests in and emerges from the relation to which the pronoun points.

The section of praise is made up of a confession of confidence (v. 5a) and a hymn of praise (vv. 5b–6). Along with his lament and cry for help, the psalmist professes his trust here and now in the very time of travail, trust in the *hesed* of the LORD, the gracious activity toward those whom God has given reason and right to call him "my God." So certain is his confidence of the reality of God's salvation that he summons his heart to sing of it (translate: "Let my heart rejoice"). The hymn lays bare the foundation upon which the whole prayer is based. Somewhere, sometime, the psalmist has encountered the graciousness of God, and confidence in that grace has become the ground and support of his life. It is the reality that no other experience can diminish and with which he undertakes to live through every other experience.

To this point the convention of referring to the one who speaks in first person in the psalm as "the psalmist" has been used. The term is a cipher for the triple identity of the psalm as event, liturgy, and scripture. The psalm's title attributes it to David, and instructs us to think about it as a prayer of his. It belongs to him as a patron of praise and prayer in the Old Testament and as the one who held the worst and best of life up to God. The full story of David's life provides a context in which the human reality of the prayer is authenticated, and his relation to the LORD stands behind its spiritual validity. The title's reference to "the choirmaster" (if that is what the

Hebrew word means) and the typical character of the prayer identify the psalm as liturgy. Its undefined specificness makes its language open to the use of many—any who take its words to express their need to the LORD. As part of the canonical collection of prayer and praise, the psalm is scripture. It is there to instruct us how to pray by disclosing to us who we are as we pray and by witnessing to us who it is to whom we pray. It is all three in unity. We reflect on the psalm as scripture to find the way to pray with David and the whole congregation of the people of God through the ages.

The psalm has no empirical proof to offer to us that the universe is not empty, void of any answer to the travail of human experience. It is simply the language of faith, but it knows what faith knows because it has already been addressed by a word, and ventures to speak because it has already heard someone "speak." The prayer, then, is witness. It testifies that God is, that he can be addressed, that one speaks to him uninhibitedly of life's worst, that he hears and accepts complaints against him for lack of attention to suffering. It is risky to think of human deprivation in terms of God's forgetting and turning away, to involve God in our imagined and real hostilities. It borders on arrogance and self-centeredness. But it is more dangerous for faith to yield to isolation, to imagine that the experience of loneliness cannot be phrased in the language of devotion.

The prayer testifies that faith may call him *"my God,"* and may dare to believe that he cares about what happens to mortals in their frailty and even has a vested interest that believers not be undone. It is risky to claim God with the possessive "my." But it is a greater error not to confess that one is God's in answer to the claim of his election. The "my" is not human initiative, but believing response based on the grace of God.

There is powerful testimony to God in what seems to be a serious inconsistency in the prayer. It speaks to God in complaint *and* in praise, speaks out of the experience of forsakenness *and* of grace, of abandonment *and* of salvation. Interpreters have sought all kinds of ways to hold the two together, to make sense of their juxtaposition. They speak of a movement of mood in which the psalmist wins his way by prayer from the darkness of despair to a joyous hope of ultimate deliverance. Or they reckon with a cultic procedure in which a response to the petition is given by a priest in the midst of the prayer, to encourage the transition. But some knew better. Luther in his exposition of the psalm calls the mood of the prayer the "state in which hope despairs, and yet despair hopes at the same time; and all that lives is 'the groaning that can be uttered,' wherewith the Holy Spirit makes intercession for us, brooding over the waters shrouded in darkness. . . . This no one understands who has not tasted it."[1]

There is a coherence that holds the apparently separate moments together. God is so much a god of blessing and salvation for the psalmist that he must speak of tribulation and terror as the absence of God. Yet God is so much the

God of *ḥesed* for the psalmist that he can speak to God in the midst of tribulation and terror as the God of his salvation. This is the deep, radical knowledge of faith, which cannot separate God from any experience of life and perseveres in construing all, including life's worst, in terms of a relation to God. It is the expression of such a powerful experience of graciousness that it refuses to see the present apart from God and cannot imagine the future apart from his salvation. "For I am sure that neither death, nor life, nor angels, nor principalities, nor things present, nor things to come, nor powers, nor height, nor depth, nor anything else in all creation, will be able to separate us from the love of God in Christ Jesus our Lord" (Rom. 8:38–39). Plaint and praise alike are the triumph of grace.

So in taking up the psalm as our prayer, we are shown who we are when we pray. We are taught our true identity as mortals, who stand on the earth and speak to a God who is ours but never owned. Agony and adoration hung together by a cry for life—this is the truth about us as people of faith. As the elect of God, we are not one but two—a duality fused and merged by the knowledge that our life depends on God. The contradiction is the enigma of the prayer, because it is the reality of faith as existence. The blessedness of this disclosure is that it strips us of all our illusions that faith is a cure, an escape from our trouble, a panacea for the awful anxiety and fear that belong to humanity. We would like to think that we begin at one end of this prayer and come out at the other, leave doubt and fear behind, and emerge in perfect trust and security. Surely faith works! Surely one day we can say "I believe" without having to cry out "LORD, help my unbelief!"

Nothing in the careers of the prophets or in the letters of the apostles or even in the life of our Lord suggests that faith works this way. In this world as it is, and in this humanity as it is, faith is more likely to bring the tears of a Jeremiah, the stigmata of a Paul, a night in Gethsemane. The psalm is not given to us to use on the rare occasions when some trouble seems to make it appropriate. It is forever appropriate for us, as long as this life shall last. We do not begin at one end and come out at the other. The agony and the ecstasy belong together as the secret of our identity. We are simultaneously the anxious, fearful, dying, historical person who cannot find God where we want him to be, and the elect with a second history, a salvation history, a life hidden with Christ in God. "How long, O LORD?" we lament into empty spaces. We also say, "You have dealt graciously with me." And all the while we pray for life in our dying, pray because through the gospel we bear already in us a foretaste of the life to come. "For while we live we are always being given up to death for Jesus' sake, so that the life of Jesus may be manifested in our mortal flesh" (2 Cor. 4:11).

## PART 3

# The Praise of the Lord

Praise the LORD!
How good it is to sing praises to our God;
　　for he is gracious, and a song of praise is fitting.
　　　　　　　　　　　　　　　　　　　—Psalm 147:1

# CHAPTER 7

# PRAISE IS FITTING
## The Psalms as Instruction in Praise

I was nurtured in an Associate Reformed Presbyterian congregation in which the Sunday service began by the people standing and singing a metrical version of the One Hundredth Psalm. The practice had a basis in the psalm itself. Psalm 100 is an entrance song, composed for a processional into the place of the Presence. It was liturgically appropriate. But I have come in retrospect to think there was more to it than mere liturgical correctness. Somewhere in the history of this practice—which, I was told, came over from Scotland with the Seceders—it had been discerned that Psalm 100 introduced the congregation to the praise of the LORD. It led the people through words that, had they ears to hear what they were singing, constituted them as what they should be and led to their doing what they should do.

Most of us in the congregation of my childhood knew the metrical psalm, versified by William Kethe, by heart:

> All people that on earth do dwell,
> Sing to the Lord with cheerful voice;
> Him serve with mirth, His praise forth tell,
> Come ye before Him and rejoice.
>
> Know that the Lord is God indeed;
> Without our aid He did us make;
> We are His folk, He doth us feed,
> And for His sheep He doth us take.
>
> O enter then his gates with praise,
> Approach with joy His courts unto;
> Praise, laud, and bless His name always,
> For it is seemly so to do.
>
> For why? The Lord our God is good,
> His mercy is forever sure;

His truth at all times firmly stood,
And shall from age to age endure.[1]

The psalm convokes us to the service of God with imperative joy, says who God is and who the congregation is, opens the gates of grace into the holy Presence, and proclaims why the LORD should be praised by a gospel of the mercy and truth of God. In the idiom of praise, the One Hundredth defines the congregation and its worship. It is liturgy that is sung torah.

I am persuaded that in a personal and local way I am talking about a much larger subject—the subject I shall try to open up in this chapter. Why is it that the psalms endured as central texts for the praise of God in Judaism and in many Christian traditions? What is at issue as so much of the church currently undertakes to revive and recover the practice of psalmody? Is it more than a fashion of the liturgical movement?

We could say the reason is simply that the psalms are in the Bible. There would be some truth to that. Such a reason was given and argued by some in sixteenth-century Geneva and Edinburgh. But this answer only pushes the question back to another level. Why these psalms, and why are any psalms there in scripture?

There is an answer to the second part of that question in the form and formation of the Psalter, the book of Psalms. As you survey the arrangement of the book, a major shift is discernible as one moves from beginning to end. In its first section the book majors in prayers in individual and corporate voice. But with the psalms numbered in the nineties a shift to hymns, the genre of praise, occurs. "Hallelujah" and "O give thanks" psalms set in and begin to predominate. Psalm 145 concludes with the personal and universal resolution: "My mouth will speak the praise of the LORD, and all flesh will bless his holy name forever" (v. 21). The psalms that follow respond to the resolution with praise of the LORD as the sovereign whose rule is known and shown in the works of creation and redemption, all to conclude with the great hallelujah of Psalm 150, which ends by calling on everything that breathes to praise the LORD. The entire *anthology* was given the name *Tehillim*, an abstract plural that means Praise. By its movement, conclusion, and title the book in its shape defines all its contents, the prayers and instruction, as the praise of the LORD. Their literary genre remains, but their function is transposed to another canonical genre. As if to be sure that the book is understood in this way, its shapers arranged that a doxology should stand at the end of each of its five sections. The making of the Psalter turns out to have been a project to put praise on the scriptural agenda. It was an enterprise that made praise canonical.

The formation of the Psalter as a project to put praise on the canonical agenda implies an answer to the first part of our double question: Why these psalms? In light of the intentionality evident in the making of the Psalter, the answer has to be something like this: Out of all the prayers and hymns and liturgies and didactic poetry composed in Israel, these tested out and proved to be the ones that enact and expound praise worthy and right for the LORD who is praised. They are the coherent response to the self-revelation of God. They are canonically commended to the people of God as praise to be learned as well as said, to be normative praise. The five books of the Psalter are a torah of praise.

So it is appropriate to ask what praise is and does in the Psalter, to ask not out of antiquarian interest, but with the understanding that our recovery of psalmody must and may be a renewal of how and why we praise the LORD. I will concentrate on three functions of psalmic praise that seem most important for our current context: praise as doxology, as confession, and as evangel.

— II —

The psalms voice and lead praise that is *doxological.* The hymns are composed and sung to give God the glory—or, better stated, to recognize and testify that the glory belongs to God. In the psalmic vocabulary, glory is the majesty, the terrible, beautiful, entrancing majesty of the all-originating and all-encompassing sovereignty of the LORD. "Who is the King of glory," the liturgy in Psalm 24 intones, this King of glory whose victory is creation and whose campaign in the world is the reign of salvation? "The LORD of hosts, he is the King of glory." In Psalm 29 "Glory" is the ecstatic cry with which the courts of heaven and the congregation on earth respond to the irresistible voice of the One who sits enthroned as king forever. Doxology is the liturgy of those who know the truth about power, because in the LORD they know the true power, the power that creates and saves.

As doxology, psalmic praise is passionately and perfectly *theological.* The term "theological" may seem both obvious and vague, and so not illuminating. Certainly in this connection it cannot mean the rational, systematic, critical discourse of the discipline traditionally called theology. The idiom of the psalms is poetry, their medium music. In an intellectual climate where there is no longer even theology in the traditional sense, but theologies *of* this and that, and theologies identified by some adjective to say what they are really about, the term alone appears incomplete. But I use it to say no more about psalmic praise than this: Its theme, its -ology, its *logos* is Adonai Elohim, the LORD God.

The subject of praise is God, nothing else. The content of the hymns in the Psalter is the knowledge of God, and all else that is mentioned in the hymns is spoken of as the knowledge of God: the cosmos, the world and all that is in it, the nations and their rulers and peoples, time, space, the soul—all is known as the knowledge of God. In only four poetic lines the One

Hundredth Psalm uses the name of God, or pronouns whose antecedent is the name, sixteen times—a not untypical concentration. Even the psalms that have the human being as topic, Psalms 8 and 139 for instance, speak of us as a way of speaking of God. The praise of God orders language to the one focus that makes speech about all else ultimately meaningful and coherent.

As doxology, psalmic praise is *the service of God*. Those who pray and praise in the psalms call themselves "the servants of the LORD." They use other self-identifications, but servant is the central one. In the Old Testament vocabulary a servant (*'ebed*) is one who belongs to a lord (*'adon*), is one whose identity and doing are given through that belonging. The public praise of God is where that identity and doing are most obvious and intentional, and is rightly called "the service of God." In their summons to worship the psalms use language that convenes the congregation for a dramatic enactment of the reign of God—servants coming into the presence of their lord to acknowledge God's rule and declare their fealty to God's reign.

In one of his homilies John Chrysostom says: "God does not need anything of ours, but we stand in need of all things from him. The thanksgiving adds nothing to him, but causes us to be nearer him."[2] That must in some senses be true; God does not need our flattery, if that be the point. But though Chrysostom said it, the caution does not address the theological reality of praise as service.

In the rabbinical tradition there is a winsome little story about the praise of God. The story tells about the time of creation. God had worked for five days and the project seemed complete. Everything seemed to be there. But to get another opinion, God consulted the attending angels. One of them very reverently pointed out that "Yes, everything was of course perfect, as was to be expected of God's own handiwork. Yet, perhaps . . . perhaps one thing could make this already perfect work more perfect: speech to praise its perfection." This seemed good to God, who thereupon created the human creature.[3]

This is, I suppose, the point at which to quote the inevitable quotation of the Westminster Shorter Catechism's definition of the purpose of the human being: "Man's chief end is to glorify God, and to enjoy him forever."

When John Calvin was commenting on the first verse of Psalm 33, which goes: "Praise is fitting for the upright," he took an ecclesiological approach to the question. "God," Calvin wrote, "creates for himself a Church in the world by gracious adoption, for the express purpose that his name may be duly praised by witnesses suitable for such a work."[4]

The rabbi sees praise as God's purpose for the human species. The Reformer sees praise as God's purpose for the church. Taken together these two doctrines say that the praise of God by the people of God is the penultimate and representative fulfillment of God's purpose for all humanity. That is why in the psalms the invocation is so often addressed to all the world.

"Acclaim the LORD, all the earth" begins Psalm 100. In the praise of God the people of God are doing what the whole world may and should do—a point to which we will return. Geoffrey Wainwright says, "Although God does not need us to be God, our praise brings the purpose of God to completion, and so is our 'duty.' "[5] The praise of God *is* the service of God; praise *is* theo-logical, in that it fulfills the purpose of God for humankind and church.

— III —

Second, psalmic praise is *confessional.* Praise as doxology declares *that* God is. Praise as confession says *who* God is. The hymns of the Psalter were Israel's confession of faith. In them the people of God said—and say—who it is they trust and obey. In the history of worship, we have come to associate the confession of faith with the literary form of the creed, but in the biblical world the congregations' declaration of whom they served took the form of praise.

Karl Barth makes a very important observation about the relation of praise and confession in the *Church Dogmatics.*[6] Praise is the larger category, of which confession is a particular expression. Hymns and creeds share the same function. The relationship needs constant attention. The church needs to take care that its hymns are as theologically right as its confession. That is one reason why psalmody deserves a regular place in the worship of the people of God. And, on the other hand, in using the creeds as statements of what we believe we must never come to think of them as being simply at our disposition. Their function as a kind of praise means they are essentially response to revelation.

The One Hundredth Psalm says, "Know that the LORD is God." That is, by the acclamation of your joyous praise, acknowledge and declare that the one who has named himself by the sacred tetragrammaton, whom the scriptures pronounce Adonai and our versions translate as LORD, that one is God, the only God, the one of whom alone the predicate God may be used, the one who in his identity defines and preempts the noun "god." And the confession is completed by declaring, "Adonai made us and we are his, his people and the sheep of his pasture." That is, the psalm adds to the confession the most central activity, which gives content to the name, the salvation-story. There you have it. Psalmic praise confesses who God is by the combination: the name and the acts and words that go with the name. In one way or another, such is the content of the hymns in the Psalter. That is also why the name of God is so important in the psalms, and can even be a surrogate for God in formulations like "Praise and bless the name of God."

There is a pertinent line in the Twenty-second Psalm. "You are holy, enthroned on the praises of Israel." Enthroned on the praises of Israel! The phrase is a revealing clue to an enigma at the heart of Israel's worship. Occasionally the psalms speak of seeing God in the sanctuary. For every other religion of the time the reference would be clear. In every sanctuary and temple there was an icon, a visible representation of the deity. But in Israel the place of the icon was vacant. The phrase "enthroned on the praises" points to what replaces the icon in Israel. The hymns of praise and the praise in the prayers render the character of God with a fullness and intentionality found nowhere else in scripture. Praise portrays the person of God by speaking of what Adonai has done and typically does, and evokes Adonai's character by a pattern of attributes. The identity that goes with the name is drawn in the praise. The throne that bears God forth as presence in Israel's worship is the praises of Israel.

This means that praise in the psalms has an iconic function. It is the liturgical obedience to the Second Commandment: "You shall not make any image or any likeness." If you asked the psalms how God is to be seen in the worship for which they are liturgy, the answer would be: by the eye of the imagination and the sense of the spirit, for the reality portrayed in praise. The content of praise creates a *verbal* icon. The psalms present the God who will not be represented by physical plastic mediums, the God who will not trust himself to the imagination and creativity of human beings. The psalms understand praise as response, the poetry of revelation. The extraordinary importance of the psalms in Israel's cult is undoubtedly a reflex of Israel's aniconic theology. Because of its representative character, Barth calls biblical praise "this little revelation on our side corresponding to God's great one."[7]

In this context we can understand why the prophets' scorn of idols is heard in the psalms.[8] Psalmic praise shares the painful knowledge that religion is a human enterprise and worship, therefore, a time of risk when praise can become betrayal. Every exercise of worship raises a question about the God whom the worshipers have in mind. "God" is a class noun, not a name, though we try to use it as such, with resulting confusion. It is easier for me to say to you within the community of faith, "My God is not like yours" than it would be to say, "My Yahweh, my Adonai, is not like yours." The name belongs to one none can own or make up.

The Form of Government of the Presbyterian Church (U.S.A.) lists as one of the basic themes of the Reformed tradition "the recognition of the human tendency to idolatry." We are incurably apt at making up our own gods to represent the concerns that drive us and the powers that are important to us. The God we worship appears in the praise we offer, so every hymnist is in danger of idolatry. A hymn by Brian Wren begins, "Bring many names" and then goes on to name (notice the verb) "God" stanza by stanza: "Strong mother God . . . warm father God . . . old aching God . . . young growing God . . . great living God."[9] The litany of names goes on until the fervor of inclusivism is satisfied, and God has passed through so many human personas that the hymn sounds like a liturgical version of Gail Sheehy's *Passages: The Predictable Crises of Adult Life.*

Re-imaging God is a perilous enterprise. Gardner Taylor puts it nicely: "Worship is a bringing the gods we make before the God who made us."[10]

The polemic against idols is, however, a minor theme in psalmic praise compared to the prominence of the negation of other gods. The hymns as Israel's confession of faith are the liturgical obedience to the First Commandment. The psalms say a "yes" to Adonai that is a "no" to other gods. When Psalm 100 says, "Adonai is God," the declaration is a denial as well as an affirmation.

There is a narrative context for this declaration in the books of Kings, where its polemical intention is very clear (1 Kings 18). The confession is the climax of the story of Elijah's contest with the prophets of Baal on Mount Carmel. When Baal failed to answer the pleading of his prophets and the LORD responded to Elijah's prayer by consuming the sacrifice, the watching assembly began to shout the confession, "The LORD is God," and the confession clearly meant that Baal was not.

The "no" to other gods is spoken in the psalms in a variety of ways. It is important to note that none of the ways is a dogmatic or theoretical monotheism. The strategy is not simply to deny the existence of other gods. They are, instead, subordinated to the kingship of Adonai and incorporated into his reign. These sentences are typical: "The LORD is the great God and a great King above all the gods" (Ps. 95:3). "All gods bow down before him" (97:7). "Who among the deities is like the LORD" (89:6). "There is none like you among the gods, O LORD. . . . You alone are God" (86:8, 10). Psalm 82 portrays a trial scene in which the gods are hauled into court, found to be failures as gods, and condemned to a human status and fate.

The thinking behind these liturgical and dramatic tactics is not so much monotheism as monotheizing. The powers and realities personalized by the gods are recognized as actual; the *good* in these powers and realities is claimed as the work of the LORD; the *idolization* of them as powers that define and order human life is denied. The deities of the ancient world were divinized powers, real powers that bore on the life of people and communities—the powers of fertility, weather, warfare, government, and the world itself. The strategy of the psalmists did not deny these powers. It rather confessed that the good the powers held for human life was the good gift of Adonai. The meaning and use of them must be ordered to the rule of Adonai.

Worship led by the psalms sets the congregation in a polytheistic world, which it claims for Adonai. Does that make it anachronistic? Some serious assessments of our culture say it is as much pagan as it is secular. The idolization of sex, wealth, patriotism, armed force, ethnicity, for example— that is, taking a good for the power that defines and orders human life— continues and revives the old paganism. Tom Wright in his incisive book *New Tasks for a Renewed Church* calls the roll of the ancient gods to name the powers of modern culture: Mars, Mammon, Aphrodite, Gaia.[11] He argues, rightly I believe, that it is urgent for the community of faith to identify the powers for what they are. You know, of course, that Gaia, the earth goddess, has been given a literary epiphany in Christian theology. The confessional situation of the church has haunting similarities to that of Israel in the eighth century and Christians in the second. Monotheizing, liberating the good realities of life and world from the perversion of divinization, is again the crucial agenda. The praise of psalms as confession is the liturgy for the mission.

I found this little story in the local section of a Nashville newspaper. A child had gotten separated from her mother in a crowded supermarket. As she searched anxiously up and down the aisles she began to cry repeatedly, "Inez, Inez." When clerks brought mother and child together, the mother asked, "Why were you calling my name? You always call me 'Mother.' " And the child said, "But, Mother, there are so many mothers in this place."

— IV —

Praise in the psalms has an *evangelical* function. Having considered the distinguishing character of praise as confession, it is important that we underscore just as clearly this other side. The praise of the people of God led by the psalms will be evangelical. Psalm 100 invites the whole earth to join its doxology, because the great Shepherd has become visible in the story of the people of God.

Hermann Gunkel, the pioneer of psalm study in the modern period, thought it unlikely that Israel would invite the world to worship the LORD on the basis of its own salvation-story. He translated the vocative in Psalm 100 (and in other similar places) as "all the land" instead of "all the earth."[12] This was one place Gunkel's historicism led him astray.

Over and over again, the hymns in the Psalter summon and invite all the nations and peoples of earth. Over and over again, they announce the reign of the LORD. "The LORD reigns; let the earth rejoice" (97:1). "Say among the nations, 'The LORD reigns.' . . . He comes to rule the earth. He will rule the world with righteousness, and the peoples with his truth" (96:10, 13). Praise is proclamation; it witnesses to the present and coming reign of the LORD. It finds in its very content the motive for its openness and outreach.

It is right to deem this proclamation "evangelical," because its content has unmistakable connections with the message of prophecy and the preaching of Jesus—indeed with the point in the record of each where *the notion of gospel* makes its definitive appearance. Isaiah 52:7: "How beautiful upon the mountains are the feet of the *mebaśśer* [the herald with good tidings], the proclaimer of shalom, the herald of good, the proclaimer of salvation, who says to Zion, 'Your God reigns.' " *Biśśer* was translated in the Septuagint by *euaggelizein,* and for all times the evangel was connected with the announcement of the reign of God. Mark 1:14–15: "Jesus came . . . preaching the evangel from and about God, saying, 'The time is fulfilled, and the kingdom of God is at hand.' " Jesus confirmed the proclamation of the reign of God as the content of the gospel. And for all time the praise of the church was connected with the proclamation of the gospel to the nations.

What this means is that the church as it praises God with the psalms is prophet and evangelist to the world around it. Its worship is to be understood as a summons to the nations to take on a different mentality ("repent") by trusting their present and future to the reign of God ("believe in the gospel"). It is no private, sectarian activity. It is public, the publication of the good news that "the LORD reigns."

The hymns in the Psalter are based on an essential theological priority. The LORD is sovereign of the world and its peoples, first of all. The dominant note is not Adonai as Israel's god, but Adonai as lord of cosmos and history. The kingdom of God is never identical with the people of God. The witness of their praise may be strange to the world, but there is no territory or population in the world that is foreign to the rule of the LORD.

It is with regard to this priority that I must enter a respectful dissent to the magisterial work of H.-J. Kraus, *The Theology of the Psalms*. He begins with a chapter on "The God of Israel" and argues that "the theology of the Psalms involves a constant effort to remain true to its subject matter—God and Israel, God and the person in Israel."[13] One is led to see the material that way if a diachronic approach is taken; that is, if one reconstructs a history of Israel's religion as the basis for setting priorities and ordering material. One begins where Israel began according to the reconstruction, and the ordering priority is set by that beginning. I have to add that it is not necessary to agree, as most do, to the reconstruction that has Israel's God graduating from a folk deity to a cosmic one by taking a degree at the old Canaanite shrine conquered by David.

But quite apart from how Israel's religion developed historically, the book of Psalms clearly focuses on Adonai as cosmic and universal sovereign. As the psalms tell it, Adonai did not become God of the world by becoming God of Israel; Adonai became Israel's God because he is God of the world and is claiming the world through his way with Israel. It is the book with its present contours and content that is our scripture and Psalter.

This theological priority has been crucial for the history of Judaism and Christianity when the two have lived and worshiped as communities in conflict with the current culture. It has crucial implications for the church in its present situation. What the church has for the world, beyond all else, is witness, witness to the God praised in our liturgy. The praise of God is the regular form of our witness in the world. As long as the church sings the psalms and praises the God envisioned in the psalms, two ways of witness are rejected.

The church that sings the psalms can never in its witness to a pluralistic world demote Adonai to just our God or one view of God or one of the gods. The church sings the psalms in the world because the God praised in them is, as the One Hundredth Psalm puts it, "the God." The witness is not a tentative proposal, subject to discussion and amendment. The witness is true, not just for the church, but for the world.

On the other hand, the church whose witness is coherent with its worship will not think and speak and act as if God's work in the world is confined to the church. God is engaged with the world in ways other than by way of the church. The witness to God in the world is possible and hopeful, because Adonai is God of the world. The liturgy calls us to look and listen and think and seek to make sense of the world beyond the church, in terms of God's sovereignty.

## — V —

There are, of course, other important purposes and characteristics of psalmic praise besides these crucial three. Psalmic praise is *joyful*. It voices an enthusiastic exuberance over the presence and steadfast love of God that ought to embarrass the faint passion of our usual congregational singing. Psalmic praise is *thankful*. It wells up from springs of gratitude for created and redeemed life. Psalmic praise is *poetic* and *musical*. Musical poetry is its proper and best medium. For that reason the metrical psalm is arguably its truest liturgical use.

Nevertheless, I have concentrated on doxology, confession, and evangelism because they resonate with the character of our times. The praise of Adonai as God, the God, the only one who can be given the predicate "god," and ultimately the one who defines God as Jesus defines Messiah/Christ, this praise of the One who has a name, a name that is self-given and identified by word and works, the praise of this God is offered in the midst of

a general religiosity that imagines the god it wants;
other religions that say who god is;
a liberal secularity that believes in no god;
a pluralism that says all gods have their rights;
a multiculturalism that relativizes gods as cultural phenomena;
a neopaganism that revives the old gods.

In such a climate, praise that is certain of its subject and confident of its purpose is called for.

In some of the prayers of the Psalter a contrast is drawn between *praise and life* on the one hand and *silence and death* on the other.[14] Praise and life are paired, and as an essential correlation stand over against silence and death. Indeed, the praise of the LORD is reckoned so valuable to the LORD that the contrast is used as the basis for a daring appeal to be heard. If the LORD does not preserve the life of those who pray, the appeal says, the LORD will lose their praise. The dead do not know or recite the wonders of divine love. So God must save life, if there is to be praise.

These prayers may seem on first reading to be no more than crass appeals to the vanity of God. But when the essential correlation between praise and life and silence and death are pondered, profound implications loom. Life is so much the gift of God's providence and salvation that it is realized only in the culmination of praise. "The living, the living, they praise you," said the prophet (Isa. 38:19). Praise is the sound of life.

Likewise the silence at issue is more than simple absence of noise or speech. The contrast identifies a special kind of silence, a dumbness before the coming and presence of the LORD. When Jesus rode into Jerusalem "humble and mounted on a donkey," the crowds broke out in praise of God with a psalm. Some Pharisees protested, and Jesus said, "I tell you, if these were *silent*, the very stones would cry out" (Luke 19:40, emphasis added). This is the special silence of which the psalms speak, and they hold it to be the symptom of death.

You can see where this essential correlation of praise and life is leading. Because praise is so much the purpose of God, and so essentially a dimension of life, death itself is on the way to being transcended. Isaac Watts discerned the inevitable implication and put it in words in his rendition of the One Hundred Forty-sixth Psalm.[15]

> I'll praise my Maker while I've breath;
> And when my voice is lost in death,
>    Praise shall employ my nobler powers.
> My days of praise shall ne'er be past
> While life and thought and being last,
>    or immortality endures.

# CHAPTER 8

# WORSHIP, WORLD, AND POWER
## An Interpretation of Psalm 100

1a        A Psalm for the Thank-Offering

b   Acclaim Yahweh, all the earth;

2a   Serve Yahweh with mirth;

b      Enter his presence with joyous shouts.

3a   Know that Yahweh is god;

b     he made us and his[1] we are;

c      his people and the flock he pastures.

4a   Enter his gates with thanksgiving,

b     his courts with praise;

c      thank him, bless his name.

5a   For Yahweh is good,

b     his loyalty is everlasting,

c      and his faithfulness lasts from generation to generation.

The most frequent action taken by a congregation of the LORD is the assembly for worship. Where questions are raised about the significance of the assembling, the One Hundredth Psalm has a right to be heard as a testimony to what the congregating is about. Were the statistics known, Psalm 100 would probably prove to be the song most often chanted throughout the history that runs from the Israelite Temple on Mount Zion to the synagogues and churches spread across the earth.[2] Many reared in the Reformed tradition of worship can hardly imagine a service that does not include "Old Hundredth." The history of the congregation that sings the psalm has carried its invitation from one place on earth out into the midst of the nations. The role the song has played in that history is evidence for the inner relation between psalm and congregation. The words of the one are the true exposition of the action of the other.

— I —

The congruence of song and service, this role of Psalm 100 as *true* explication of the congregation, is a presupposition of the history in which the hymn has moved from Jerusalem Temple to Christian church. For this particular psalm, the Old Testament–New Testament hermeneutical problem hardly exists. The Christian interpreter who works through its measures meets almost no resistance to understanding the gathering of the church through its images and ideas. Indeed, he uncovers the structure of signifi-

72

cance in the assembly described in the psalm that binds him to the synagogue as one branch of the community whose historic origins run through Zion. Of course, the psalm was written with a specific congregation in mind, and shows that in its language. But it was composed as though it was meant to be open to future times and other places, and lays only the lightest foundation in its historical time and place.

*Who sings this hymn?* The psalm does not at first say specifically, and thereby lets it be known that the singers' willingness and capacity to say, "Acclaim Yahweh, all the earth" is enough to know about them. The singers become visible concretely only in the first-person pronouns of verse 3b, which are syntactically bound to the name "Yahweh." They are the people whom Yahweh brought into existence as a people, over whom he has creator's rights. Whoever can say that can sing the psalm.

*Where do the singers stand?* They stand not just anywhere, but at a very particular place, specifically at the entrance to the courts of the Temple in Jerusalem (v. 4ab). Yet the space where the action to which the psalm summons can occur is not necessarily local, but personal. It is the possessive adjectives in verse 4ab that are definitive: *"his* gates . . . *his* courts" (emphasis added). The crucial determination of "the place where" has already been set in 2b: "enter *his presence"* (emphasis added). The place of the presence in Old Testament and New is not irrevocably fixed on a map; it depends on the LORD's will to be accessible to people. But the confidence that he is accessible within space, that by his condescension to our history and lives he himself does establish "presence"—that confidence underlies the whole song. The right context, then, the place where the song is at home, is where folk who know their identity in relation to the one named Yahweh form themselves in response to his presence.

— II —

In order to understand *the words* as explication of the assembly's reality, the psalm's history as burden has to be overcome. The very frequency of the song's use has worn its phrases to smooth familiarity. The psalm as a composition is a work of tradition, art, and faith. The presence and role of all three have to be recognized and respected if the theological work that created the psalm is to be appreciated. The one who created its four lines (vv. 1b–2ab, 3, 4, 5) was not only a skilled poet; this poet knew how to select the basic phrases of faith and culture and how to weave them together in a pattern that comes as near as possible to serving as a theological paradigm for the occasion on which the song was to be sung. The language does strike anyone accustomed to the Old Testament as the usual sort of thing;[3] the poem can be passed over as hardly more than an artful weaving together of the customary from the reservoir of the traditional cultic speech.[4] But that would mistake its genius. The "customary" words are the loaded words—the sounds that have by a long history acquired the capacity of symbols to carry the burden of faith's meaning. They are not used casually, but in a careful precision that aims at maximum significance crafted into chiseled brevity. Moreover, into the arrangement of the text subtle but powerful variations on the expected have been wrought so as to give the four poetic lines a personality and individuality all their own.

The psalm is a variation and amplification of a basic hymn formula, which "appears so frequently that it is one of the surest and most easily recognized characteristics of the hymn."[5] The formula has two elements. The first is the introductory summons to praise; the second is an assertion about Yahweh introduced by "for" (*ki*), which states the basis for the summons and thus the actual content of praise. The essential formula is apparent in passages like Exodus 15:21:

> Sing to Yahweh, for he has triumphed gloriously;
> the horse and the rider he has thrown into the sea.

The presence of the formula as the structure of verses 4 and 5 is obvious. Three imperatives call for the assembly to proceed into the sanctuary, all the while praising Yahweh (v. 4); and then the basis and content of the phrase is asserted: "for Yahweh is good" (v. 5). Indeed, the composer has used a specific version of this hymn formula as the basis for these two lines.[6] Verses 4 and 5 are simply an amplification of the short *Todah*-hymn:[7] "Thank Yahweh, for he is good; for his loyalty is everlasting." The use and distribution of the *Todah*-hymn in the Psalter and in the Chronicler's history[8] indicates the important role that it played in Israel's cult. In the postexilic period it became the central liturgical utterance of the congregation. By its use as the basis of the final two lines of the psalm, the composer establishes the purpose of the whole. Its words are the spiritual pilgrimage-way for those who go to give thanks; and what that means for them is apparent when the relationship of "thanksgiving" to the intention of the entire psalm is understood.[9]

The composition of the first two lines invites the conclusion that the hymn formula has been used as structure there also, so that the whole is made up of a twofold repetition of this basic movement.[10] The opening line (1b–2ab) does consist of three imperative sentences, and so corresponds to the first element of the formula. The mind and ear attuned to the logical sequence of summons and reason expects to say and hear, "For Yahweh is indeed god." Instead, there follows a fourth imperative, "Know," followed indeed by *ki*, but with a different meaning ("that"). So the second element of the formula does not appear; it is displaced by an imperative that continues the first line in such a way that, instead of hearing the basis of praise, one encounters an unexpected extension of the first element. This fourth imperative sentence gathers up and interprets the preceding three. The inference of the sequence is that acclaiming and serving and appearing before Yahweh is a way of "knowing" that he is god; verse 3 defines the theological intention of the actions commanded in the first line.

To achieve this effect the composer has not had to create verse 3a. The imperative sentence "Know that Yahweh is indeed god" is a variation on the "recognition formula."[11] In its general use in the language of Israel's faith, the formula is always set after a reference to an act of Yahweh and expresses the goal and confirmation of the event: " . . . and you [he, they] will know that I am Yahweh." The imperative form of "know" and the formulation of the object-sentence as an assertion of Yahweh's exclusive right to the predicate "god" are similar to uses of the formula in Deuteronomic texts.[12] By introducing an imperative version of the formula as a continuation of the opening imperatives that summon to specific responses, the composer gives a theological intention to these responses and relates them, not to the congregation itself, but to an initiative of Yahweh; the invitation is not based in the congregation, but in the one to whom the invitation points. The *Todah* theme of verses 4 and 5 is in fact prepared for by establishing what the "thanking" is about.

— III —

Line 1 (1b–2ab) announces a bold invitation! Three parallel imperative sentences repeat the summons in close synonymity; yet each advances and develops the significance of the summons. The line specifies the addressees of the invitation, designates whom the invitation concerns, and describes the activity in which the invitees are to join. The addressees of the summons are the inhabitants of *all the earth*.[13] The command is meant to be universal. This is no choir calling only to Israelites within the sound of its voice; the sequence of imperatives reaches out to humankind. Of course, the call cannot be heard at such a range; there is no practical way to effect communication with all people, or any means to make them listen. Whenever the psalm is sung, the words go out no farther than any other human words, and yet the vocative "all the earth" is inescapably necessary. What the singers undertake has to do with the world, and should their horizon be at all foreshortened the happening would immediately decay into something else. Against all practicality or human expectation of being heard, they summon humankind. They await no eschatological climax of history to make certain that the time will be ripe for such a venture, nor do they measure their words against their resources and possibilities. No, they look to him who is the focus of what they undertake and shout "all the earth," because no lesser assembly can be contemplated where he is concerned. What they gather to do must always be set in the midst of the world, or it is surrender of truth and future from the start.

The invitation concerns *Yahweh*. It would be easy to pass by the name without notice; it is expected and can be taken for granted. But the psalmist has done everything within the capacity of art to rivet attention beyond all else on the name. In four poetic lines the name is uttered four times, and in every measure lacking the name it is represented by an echoing pronoun—as if to say this identity is so urgently important that no sentence can be spoken without some word that represents it. Whatever else this activity may mean, it is a relationship to the bearer of this name, and it is to Yahweh that humanity is called. Here at first nothing is said about this name to lend identity or character to it. That will happen later, when Yahweh is the subject of two declarations ("Yahweh is god" . . . "Yahweh is good"). But initially the name stands on its own, because it is a personal name, which by its nature designates one in distinction from others. Yahweh is not god in general. He is not identified or categorized by ideas or deeds done by others. He is not to be confused or merged with the sources of other deeds and words. He is Yahweh.

The form and style of the activity proposed in the imperative sentences is *political;* the language belongs to the monarchical frame of reference and draws its basic meaning from that sphere. This is not obvious to us, because in the course of its history this particular terminology has come to be defined by presuppositions that wall off such assemblies from what is recognized as political. These terms, as the handbooks usually remark, belong to Israel's cultic vocabulary, and designate the kind of things that Israel, and other peoples of the culture area, were accustomed to do in the public cult. They would form processions before the gates of the sanctuary area and enter its precincts, where the deity was believed to dwell or come, all the while lauding him with epithets and affirmations. But cult in Israel's cultural world was not a self-contained and self-defining sphere. All these actions had meaning, because they were expressed in the forms by which a people recognized the One who wielded power over them.

The second imperative sentence (v. 2a) guarantees that the royal setting is in view here. A superficial use of the lexicons might suggest that "serve" (*'abad*) is no more than "customary cultic language,"[14] but a closer inspection of its usage in the Psalter shows that here it specializes in one of its possible functions, denoting the conduct appropriate for relation to a royal figure.[15] "Serve Yahweh" is a command that holds the action in the political context and should be heard as an interpretation of cult, rather than the other way around. The two areas of the Old Testament tradition in which *'abad* clusters are not without significance for the psalm. In the exodus tradition it designates the goal of leaving pharoah's domain to go into the wilderness;[16] "serving Yahweh" is clearly the alternative to remaining the slaves of Egypt's king. Unless its political dimension is observed, the significance of the exodus tradition is obscured. The verb also accumulates in Deuteronomic paraenesis,[17] where it connotes the relationship to "other gods" and "Yahweh." Again an alternative is involved, this time between deities; serving

Yahweh excludes the granting of an authoritative role to another deity. Together the two clusters show that to serve Yahweh is conduct that excludes slavery to human government or subjection to the power of the "gods." So "serve Yahweh" says how the context of cultic activity is to be understood and what the character of the visible activity actually is. Seen from its perspective, the other commands fall into place. "Come before him . . ." is entry into the sanctuary, but the language is also used for audience before a human king.[18] The acclaiming shout of the congregation is "religious praise," but in the rituals of political life one shouts acclaim (the *teru'ah*) to the king when he appears.[19]

The invitation is a summons to activity whose nature and intention is the formation of a congregation as the realm of Yahweh.[20] It can be called worship because its focus is god; but its rubrics and movements and responses come from the political life of human society, because it is the recognition by humans of the locus of power. The royal sociology of Israel's day has little contemporary currency. But the actuality of power, the problem of power structures, and the political reality of both abide. Therefore the assembly that the psalm convokes cannot lose its political dimension if it is to fulfill its intention. The psalm belongs at the point where mortals publicly assemble to recognize the power to which they will submit their living. It means opting for one "power structure" as decisive, and therefore it ought to be the most significant social action that human beings can take.

— IV —

Where the first three imperative sentences establish the social sphere whose rubrics lend form and meaning to the event of worship, the fourth (v. 3a) moves on to the inner significance of the act. The invitation to "know that Yahweh is god" gathers up and interprets the meaning of the first three. To elaborate the interpretation through the invitation, the psalmist has chosen to use a hortatory formulation of the "recognition formula," whose dimensions of meaning in the theological tradition of Israel come into play here. The knowledge involved is less cognition than recognition. In the most frequent use of the formula, it was the perception of Yahweh's identity in response to a sign, primarily an act in history.[21] This knowing cannot be self-generating— that is, an experience of the enthusiasm and emotion that the congregation works up in itself by its own doing. Nor can this knowing be a personal blending with the divine, realized mystically through the cultic space where the *deus praesens* is intense. The command to know depends on and presupposes Yahweh's initiative, that he has acted in such a way as to call for the appropriate corresponding response.[22]

The content of the recognition is a confessional sentence: "Yahweh is god!" Obviously, this is by its form a declaration said not *to* Yahweh, but *about* him, and therefore to others. It is testimony and proclamation. The confessional character of the sentence—and the character of the confession—are shown by its use in the story of Elijah's contest with the prophets of Baal on Mount Carmel. In response to the sign of the divine fire, the assembly of the people, who had heretofore vacillated between allegiance to Yahweh and allegiance to Baal, shouted, "Yahweh is God! Yahweh is God!" (1 Kings 18:39). The wonder resolved the uncertainty into which Israel had fallen and brought the congregation to the faith voiced in the declaration.

This particular confession has the character of a choice, a recognition that excludes other options. It bears both a polemical and a constructive moment. All sources of power and authority but one are denied; it always means a theological rejection of every identity not named in the sentence. And one is recognized and affirmed absolutely—the one whose personal name is the subject of the sentence. The predicate "god" is completely preempted by Yahweh. This type of confession (like the New Testament's "Christ is Lord") belongs to the polytheistic or, better, the polydynamistic situation. The subject, rather than the predicate, is the issue; no ontological problem is involved in the category "god." The term is completely functional, has to do with who and what demands and deserves the ultimate allegiance and attention of mortals. This confession is quite unlike statements about the existence of god, or statements that attribute qualities to god as a way of giving content to the category, of defining its actuality. Its concreteness lies in the proper name whose authenticity and appropriateness depend on its connection with quite particular and specific words and deeds, which are there in space and time over against those who make confession. The elements of the encounter in the Elijah story are obvious; what they are in the psalm—that of which the confession speaks in uttering the name Yahweh—is established in v. 3bc.

Alongside the confession, the composer has set two echoing cola in parallelism. They are not merely synonymous; they pick up the name Yahweh in the confessional sentence and, by using it as subject of a verb (*he* made us) and as a possessive (*his* we are, *his* people and the flock of *his* pasture), testify to the way in which the identity that bears the name has been disclosed to Israel. The "making" is not the creating of the world and its creatures, but the historical fashioning of the worshiping community.[23] The sentence is the shortest possible expression for the holy history by which Yahweh chose and called and saved a people so that there might be a folk on earth who know his name and acknowledge his rule. That the maker owns what he fashions is a principle of the most primitive logic. The metaphor of "making" for the historical tradition of Yahweh's deeds leads naturally into the acknowledgment that the congregation is "his people." And the psalmist adds the favorite image of the shepherd and his flock to draw out the feeling of being led and cared for that complements the highly compressed confession of origin and identity. So the verb speaks of the deed on which existence rests and the possessive of the relationship that defines existence. In contrast to the initial confession, which speaks only of Yahweh, the testimony now includes a reference to the congregation. In confessing the identity of the one who alone owns the predicate "god," the worshiping community must and does speak of itself. "Yahweh is god" means that he is the maker and possessor of those confessing; the sentence shows that "god" is a word with which the congregation points to the source of its existence and identity. The identity and existence of God and congregation are indissolubly united. In praise, one speaks of oneself in speaking of God, or the term is emptied of any possible significance.

The psalm shows no embarrassment or hesitation in having the congregation speak of its own origin and identity in summoning all the earth to acknowledge that Yahweh is god. In fact they have no other option. They know Yahweh's identity only through the deeds and words of his history with them; they can point to him in no other way. To attempt another option would in the end be to speak of some other identity. On the other hand, to invite the world to acknowledge that Yahweh is god means that the congregation knows that its own creation and identity do not exhaust Yahweh's role as god nor limit his purpose in dealing with them. The flock is a sign to all mankind concerning the shepherd, the constant invitation that points away from itself to the shepherd, the possibility for life within another power structure, different from all the others already experienced and known by mortals.

— V —

In verse 4 the psalmist intensifies the invitation, and in verse 5 finally states the basis of the summons. To do so he has, as observed above, used the basic *Todah*-hymn and amplified both its elements. Its imperative ("thank Yahweh") has been expanded to an entire poetic line so that the *Todah* motif can assume its rightful place as the final definition of the assembly's action. The theme appears both in the noun *todah* and the verb *hodu*, for which "with praise" and "bless his name" are simply synonyms. We are accustomed to translate these words by "thanksgiving" and "thank." But something fundamental escapes the necessities of translation in this case. The Hebrew language had no precise equivalent for our word "thank"; and the action designated by the verb and noun was qualitatively different.[24] In our culture the one who thanks is himself the subject of the act ("I thank you") and, though he responds with the expression to another, he remains more or less apart. The attitude of the word is undefined, and may run from real gratitude to casual politeness; the expression can even voice frigid hostility and create personal distance. In the act of *todah*, that is impossible, because here in what is said the other is always subject of the speech. *Todah* is in fact praise, sentences that speak with exuberance of what the other does and is, affirmations that articulate dependence. "With this *hodu* we are not called to a sentence in which *I* am the subject, but to one in which *God* is the subject."[25] Therein lies the appropriateness of the title's classification of the psalm, *letodah;* it is from beginning to end a summons to that kind of action. Line 1 calls for a dramatic actualization of the sentence: Yahweh is king; line 2 interprets that drama as an assertion that Yahweh alone is god; line 4 declares that Yahweh is good. What is intended is living, public confession in the form of praise, theology in corporate social formation. It is all the translation into visibility and audibility of the government that has claimed the congregation.

*Hodu* as a definition of what we call worship sets a severe limit on the possibilities of our performance. The congregation invites and acts, but it can never become either source or object of what is done. It does not offer itself to the world. It does not build the kingdom that it dramatizes. It does not celebrate or seek victories of its own. It knows the subtle danger of "I believe in the holy catholic church" said in isolation, and understands the temptation in slogans like "Let the church be the church." Ultimately, with its "thanking" response it will—and can—say only, "Let the LORD be the LORD." But because this is so, the limitation is really a liberation. The thanking occasion is the place where mortals can cease the feverish "making themselves" and begin "receiving themselves" as a gift, the time when all are set free from all powers that restrict and reduce them because they are found by a power that is for them.

— VI —

It is only in his amplification of the second part of the *Todah*-hymn that the composer finally makes the transition to the second element of the basic formula and introduces the declarations that announce what is both content of the praise and the basis and reason for the imperatives. By sustaining the imperatives so long without transition to the anticipated "for" sentence, he gives the final line an even more climactic emphasis. The nominal sentences in verse 5ab are essentially a verbatim use of the short *Todah*-hymn's second element; the psalmist has added "Yahweh" to reintroduce the central identity not mentioned by name since 3a and to achieve a two-beat colon; the second "for" which usually precedes "everlasting his loyalty" has been dropped to bring the sentence into a more direct synonymous parallel with the first, so that it clearly appears as an interpreting echo of the predicate "good." Verse 5c then furnishes a synonymous parallel with 5b; "faithfulness" is used so often as a word-pair with "loyalty" in the phraseology of the Psalter that it functions as a hendiadys meaning "faithful loyalty"; it offers the inescapable predicate with which to form the final colon.

Why should a congregation form itself as a procession of those who thereby choose and profess the reign of Yahweh? Not simply because he is god, and therefore has status that demands the submission and glorification of mortals—or any variant of that answer, such as that he holds all power, or is wrathful against opposition. Such answers are at times given in scripture and have their validity. But the answer given here—the primary answer without which the others lose their ultimate cogency, failing above all to loose joy and exaltation among mortals, the first answer of Israel by right of its place in the basic hymn—is that Yahweh is good (*tob*). The word is so common and broad as to seem a faded and feeble generality. Yet it is precisely because of its inevitability in human speech and its inclusiveness in range of function that it is the right predicate for Yahweh. In their languages, human beings organize their discriminating responses to what they experience in every sphere of life with the word-pair "good" and "bad," calling "good" that which best brings to consummation their existence within any particular sphere. In this declaration "good" designates Yahweh as the one who, within the sphere of relationships to other persons and powers, confirms and sustains and fulfills personal existence. The predicate was so appropriate and authentic for Yahweh that later Judaism came to be apprehensive about its general use and jealous of Yahweh's prerogatives with respect to it. Jesus asks, "Why do you call me good? No one is good but God alone."[26] "He is good"—that is the primary basis for the worship of Yahweh, and the underlying meaning of every utterance of praise.

The word is not left without a contextual guide to how the congregation knows the good of Yahweh and how they understand it. There is an interpretive clue in the use of the *Todah*-hymn of which the adjective is a constituent element. Within the Psalter the *Todah*-hymn appears primarily as a structural feature of "historical hymns," which survey the items of the traditional salvation-history as the content of praise;[27] once it frames the "thanksgiving of an individual" who celebrates the deliverance Yahweh has worked for him;[28] and another time it introduces a long series of strophes celebrating Yahweh's saving answer to people in a variety of troubles.[29] In Jeremiah 33:11, it is the hymn that will be sung after the exile by those who bring "thank offerings" to Yahweh's Temple when he has "restore[d] the fortunes of the land as at first." Without exception, the short hymn belongs to the praise of those who have been saved. Whether it be the great congregation who know that their existence in every generation is a manifestation of the redemption from Egypt, or the individual who experiences that salvation in his own deliverance, or the exiles who find in the return a recapitulation of that salvation—the assurance and understanding of Yahweh's goodness are the same. He saves! He brings the history of people and the lives of individuals through. And praise is the expression of the life and joy one would not have apart from his work.

The word for that work expressed in such a way is loyalty (*ḥesed*), and by the use of that word as the elaborating parallel to "good," a second and concurring interpretation is given. In the Psalter's vocabulary of praise, *ḥesed* is the characterizing term for Yahweh's salvation; for example, "Yahweh has made known his salvation. . . . He has remembered his *ḥesed* and faithfulness to the house of Israel" (Ps. 98:2–3). The word is tantalizingly impossible to reproduce in English. In its secular use it designated the character of an act that lived up to and vindicated the responsibilities of a given relationship to the benefit of the other.[30] In Israel, with its election theology, the word became a crucial theological instrument to describe Yahweh's benevolent deeds for those to whom he was related. In the laments and petitions of those in trouble, it was the *ḥesed* of Yahweh for which they prayed; Yahweh's *ḥesed* is the "favor" he shows to those who, turning to him in the anxieties and uncertainties of their human situation, call him "my god." In Yahweh's *ḥesed* lies the basis for trust (Ps. 13:6) and hope (Ps. 130:7). Because the possibility of living in trust and hope is created by Yahweh's *ḥesed*, it is the fundamental reality of his "good."

The synonyms "everlasting" and "from generation to generation" establish a temporal perspective for the declaration of the basis of praise. These phrases reach out to include the furthest extent of time, saying that Yahweh's *ḥesed* will be coextensive with history. The knowledge of Yahweh's *favor* comes through traditions of the past, ever renewed by recurrences of that *ḥesed* in the present. But that knowledge does not turn back to the past; it summons to the future. The basis of praise is the confidence that the LORD's faithful favor in the past has already opened up the future as the sphere of his goodness. From the vantage of worship one cannot see the detailed *what* of the future, but the congregation can behold *who* waits there. Praise grows out of, and begins to actualize in the present, the vision of the goodness of the LORD, which awaits the worshiping community in the tomorrows of life.

— VII —

In the face of widespread doubt that the congregation's most frequent action is also its most important—indeed, is important at all—the psalm insists that *the assembly defined by its intention* has significance for all of history. It lays down that claim with the boldness of its opening invitation: "Acclaim Yahweh, all the earth!" Those who sing the song dare to presume that all people should join in what they do. They point to one focus as the source of life and the object of life's enthusiasm, thereby subordinating all other sources and objects of the joy of existence. Such an invitation, wholeheartedly given and profoundly meant, is the offer of a way to know truth and to respond to goodness. To know the truth and respond to goodness is the essential business of life.

The question is whether the invitation is still announced by the congregation in boldness and seriousness—whether those who make it heard now really mean to be heard in all earnestness, because they believe and know with great joy that their visible assembly points to truth and responds to goodness. Against the congregation's uncertainty, the psalm stands as a gift of grace—the opportunity to recover the authenticity of the accustomed act. True, the song's paradigmatic character and repeated use always pull toward the commonplace. In the midst of a congregation whose sense of identity and purpose have faded to neutral habit, the familiar basic phrases can become echoes of the meaninglessness of this environment. In its metrical versions and role in the liturgy, the psalm can turn into the routine words of a routine cult. This context then determines the content, and gives the clues for understanding to those who speak and to those who listen. Yet in the boldness and seriousness of the very words there abides a power that will not settle into this banality, a vigor that constantly overbids timid meanings and passive repetition to draw those who sing the words back into the venture that is their original and authentic context: "Know that Yahweh is God indeed!"

## PART 4

# David as Psalmist and Messiah

Of David. A Miktam, when the Philistines
seized him in Gath.
— Psalm 56, superscription

I have found my servant David;
with my holy oil I have anointed him.
— Psalm 89:20

# CHAPTER 9

# THE DAVID OF THE PSALMS

Selecting a subject like "the David of the Psalms" is a sign of what is going on in biblical studies in our time. The subject *suggests* that there is a David whose reality and importance lie in his connection with psalms and psalmody. The subject *assumes* that it is legitimate and useful to be interested in this figure who exists as a literary reality—and may never have existed in any other way. The subject is *a way of claiming* that such a figure is a proper matter for Old Testament study and research.

Such suggestions, assumptions, and claims are symptomatic of the change in the climate of biblical studies. In mainstream historical-critical studies of the past era, such suggestions, assumptions, and claims would have been generally suspect, and in many quarters vehemently rejected. The regnant and normative question has been the historical one—and history has been understood as historicity. Was the historical David a psalmist? Did he write the psalms attributed to him? If not, how did his connection with the psalms arise? The answers to these questions that have been thought most probably correct have separated the psalms from David, and have largely dismissed "the David of the Psalms" as a subject of valid study.

In the context of current Old Testament study, in contrast, there is a new and unapologetic interest in the investigation of such subjects as "the Jeremiah of the Book," "the Moses of Deuteronomy," and "the David of the Psalms." This interest does not amount to a rejection of the historical-critical studies of the past, or of their results. It is, rather, based on a perception that using only one way to question the material does not do justice to its character and purpose as text, nor does it serve adequately the uses of the texts by the social groups that read and transmit them. There is a new appreciation of the value of tradition and its role in the intellectual world of social groups. There is a renewed understanding of the capacity of literature to shape and re-create reality. (Scarlett O'Hara is more real as a fact of culture than countless women in Atlanta whose names and addresses are listed in the telephone book.)

There is a new vision of the canonical process and the canonical shape of biblical literature as the normative and claiming dimension of the text.

Some want to speak of what is emerging as a "postcritical" era. I am uneasy about using the notion, because it can so easily be misunderstood. Criticism, in the best and right sense, is not past. Criticism is simply a procedure for clearing the mind to see what is there. The historical-critical question has been asked and much learned. It cannot be forgotten. The lesson has been, to sum it up in a rather presumptuous way: *avoid genre confusion*. But it has been the broadening and the development of critical practice that has put tradition, literature, and canon in focus. Biblical criticism is not outmoded; if it were, then the assiduous and difficult work of submitting the mind to the text, the project of seeing what is there, the goal of assessing the text's reality in ways appropriate to its genre—all that would be lost. That is not what is happening in contemporary biblical studies. To take "the David of the Psalms" as one's theme is symptomatic of these developments in the discipline and its understanding of its task.

The David of the Psalms has always been an important feature of the church's traditional understanding of scripture, liturgy, and prayer. Prompted by the way in which David and the psalms are connected in the Old Testament canon, Christians have understood David in terms of the Psalms and have viewed the psalms as belonging to David. Because Christians have continuously used the psalms as the core of their praise and prayer, and in doing so have believed that David was both type and prophet of the Christ, the David of the Psalms has had an immense influence on Christian belief and practice. The psalmic David remains more real for most Christians than the David of history, and probably even than the David of the Samuel story.

Among the memorabilia of my youth is a book with the title *The Harp of David*. It is a psalter, arranged for choral singing, that was once widely used in Presbyterian congregations. As we sang these psalms, we had David's story to give them human and dramatic context, and because we understood that his life and words were typical and prophetic of Christ, we understood why we were singing these songs and what they meant in the context of Christian worship. David was the sweet psalmist of Israel. The songs that came out of his life as shepherd and warrior, as refugee and ruler, were the inspired expression of a life devoted to God in bad times and good, and therefore the guiding language for all who undertook lives of devotion. He was the chosen of the Lord, the messiah. His relation to the psalms rendered them "messianic," songs that not only expressed his and our praise and prayer, but at their deepest level spoke of the one who for us was the Christ.

This David of the Psalms was, of course, part of our heritage. He is to be found in every era of Christian tradition. The picture is varied by the different imaginations and concerns of changing history. But the picture is consistent in its essentials and function. Tracking the subject through the eras of liturgy and interpretation simply turns up historical variations of the basic image. It is already present early in the Common Era in distinctive forms in Christianity and Judaism.

For the rabbis, David was almost exclusively the psalmist, so much so that all the psalms were ascribed to him, who composed them under the inspiration of the Shekinah.[1] His life was one of unceasing praise and thanksgiving to God, nothing more than a context for all the psalms.[2] And he was, says Sirach, one who not only lived a life of praise, but founded the observance of psalmody and the occasions for its use in the life of Israel (Sir. 47:8–10). These references are only hints of the degree to which David and the psalms are subjects that had been collapsed into each other.

The fathers of the postapostolic age regularly mentioned David in two coordinate roles: he is the singer of the psalms and the prophet of Christ.[3] It is this latter role which preoccupies the writers of the New Testament. In the key texts on the matter, it is made clear that in such psalms as 110, David is inspired to speak, not of himself, but of the Christ (Mark 12:35–37; Matt. 22:43–45; Luke 20:41–44). David is a prophet, and the book of Psalms is the collection of his inspired sayings that illuminate the Christ-event and matters connected with it, a position that fits into the common view in the New Testament of the nature and use of the Old Testament scriptures (Acts 1:16–20; 2:25–35; 4:25; Rom. 4:6–8; 11:9–10; Heb. 4:7). In the New Testament, interest in David as source of psalmody and liturgy for the community seems marginal, but it is important to remember that the emphasis that is present is the basis for the use of the psalms in the liturgy of the early church. The psalms were used, and were understood as they were, because of their connection through David with Christ.

The Dead Sea Psalms Scroll shows the interest at Qumran in the notion of the David of the Psalms.[4] The scroll reflects the most fully developed phase of the tradition known from the ancient world. David is said to have composed four thousand and fifty psalms and to have provided songs for all the occasions in the cultic calendar. All the psalms were spoken through prophecy given him by God. The scroll contains two, perhaps three, psalms composed to go with occasions in David's life known from the books of Samuel (Pss. 152, 153, and 151B). There is even a suggestion in Psalm 151A that the practice of psalmody in his youth was a human basis for David's selection by God, a kind of merit which justified the divine choice.

The notion of the "David of the Psalms" has its defining and orienting origin in the Old Testament. The question can be asked whether a descriptive and constructive look at it in that context can contribute to its understanding and use today. There is no need to look again at the history of the notion. Questions about whether David composed any of the psalms, or which psalms, and what basis there is in fact for the connection between David and psalmody, have probably been pressed to their useful limits. The various conclusions reached have, of course, always been less than the tradition claimed. The purpose here is, rather, to ask what implications about the character and use of the idea can be drawn by looking at it in its literary context in the Old Testament.

The contexts are several. David is connected with the psalms in the books of Samuel, Chronicles, and Psalms. As one looks at these textual areas, it quickly becomes clear that nothing like the full traditional notion of the David of the Psalms is present in any one of them. One must look in turn at all three and ask in what way each stands in relation to the others. The Old Testament "David of the Psalms" is a notion to which there are three different witnesses.

## The Books of Samuel

At the beginning of his story in Samuel, David appears as a musician. According to 1 Samuel 16:14–23, he was discovered in the talent hunt for a lyrist who would play for Saul when the evil spirit came upon him. "So," P. Kyle McCarter says, "according to the oldest tradition available to us, David came to the court as a musician and royal weapon bearer."[5] The lyre (*kinnor*) was the noblest instrument in the culture, and it is as a skilled performer on it that David appears in this story (see also 19:9 and the doublet in 18:10). One would like to imagine that David sang one of the individual laments for Saul, the psalm of a person in trouble. But the descriptions of David's performance suggest that he only made music with the lyre; four times the expression "played with his hand" is used. In Israel, as in all the ancient world, musicians were not recreational entertainers in any modern sense. Music had a role and function in relation to the needs and important occasions of social life. Its four primary settings in early Israel seem to have been social celebration, warfare, incantation, and cultic rituals.[6] As the story makes clear, David serves as an exorcist of Saul's evil spirit, using melody as power against the possession. To what uses David had been putting his skill before he came to court, the story does not say. In any case, the connection in the earliest tradition is with music, but not yet psalmody.

In 2 Samuel 6:1–19, David brings the "ark of God, which is called by the name of the LORD of hosts who sits enthroned on the cherubim," from its exile in previously Philistine territory. By this act David introduces the God of Israel into the new royal city, and in effect provides for the national cult that will be centered in Jerusalem. On the occasion he was also performing in and leading the elaborate ritual celebrations that accompanied the transfer (vv. 5, 15). This ritual relocation of the Ark assumes that David would have provided for an ongoing cult centered in the Ark, but the narrator is not concerned with these particulars. We will hear of them from Chronicles. That a king of Israel should be active in founding, organizing, and participating in the central cult is quite expected in terms of what we know about the role of rulers in that time. That the king would be a participant, a singer, a player is, on the other hand, quite special, a particular that marks the David of Samuel.[7]

The narrative in the books of Samuel includes the texts of three poems sung by David: one just before he was made king of Judah, one at the climax of his career, and one as his swan song.

Second Samuel 1:17–27 is the beautiful *qina* over the slain Saul and Jonathan. The probability that it was composed by the historical David is greater than for any other song in the Old Testament. The introduction to the dirge tells about it two interesting things whose implications are important for our subject. David ordered the dirge to be taught to the people of Judah, presumably to memorialize Saul and Jonathan; David is shown as creator and patron of national music. The song was written in the Book of Jashar (perhaps, according to a Greek textual tradition, "the Book of Song"); the narrator knows that a song attributed to David was transmitted as part of a collection whose text was fixed in writing.

Second Samuel 22 is a song of David that praises the LORD for his deliverance from his enemies (vv. 2–20), thus vindicating his righteousness before the LORD (vv. 21–28), and for his prowess as a warrior, by which he has achieved dominion over the nations (vv. 29–51). This long, complex song makes two major contributions to the David–Psalms relationship. First, it provides a "psalmic perspective" on the entire career of David. The introduction to the song (v. 1), a summary report provided by the narrator who put the psalm in its present place in the book, says David addressed this song to the LORD in a time when the LORD delivered David from the power of all his enemies and from Saul. The song of praise thus stands as theological commentary on the long story of David's struggles with Saul and with the foes of Israel, a story that in its telling usually goes without theological construal. The reader is asked to think of each episode and of the whole in terms of the LORD's deliverance, a vast witness to the covenant loyalty of the LORD to his anointed king (see v. 51). The conclusion of the song even gives it a dimension of prophecy, by saying that this history of *hesed* will be the future of David's "seed forever," making David's story pattern and type of what is to be. Because the song is a case of genre, motifs, and ideas that typify the Psalter, it is the hermeneutical door in the narrative for the use of psalms in general as context for reading the David story.

Second, the song establishes in the canon a Davidic view of the psalms. It is the earliest literary evidence of a connection between David and the psalms, and the only specific witness in the David story to that relationship. The song appears as Psalm 18 in the book of Psalms, with the narrative introduction composed for its setting in Samuel. Its earliest extant literary use is in the story, but the narrator who put it in its place must have known it as "Davidic." Perhaps it or its major components were part of a "*ledawid*" collection current in Jerusalem. As one of the psalms in the growing canonical collection, this psalm inevitably pointed to a narrative setting in David's life for other *ledawid* psalms, and may have given some impetus to the production of the other different settings of psalms in the narrative of Samuel.

Second Samuel 23:1–7 reports "the last words of David" in the form of a poem, which also has two points of interest for our subject. According to the traditional translation, the introduction (v. 1) identifies David as "the sweet psalmist of Israel" (so RSV). But the Hebrew *zemirot* is not the usual word for psalm, and there is some textual support for pronouncing the consonants as the singular form of a divine epithet, with a resulting meaning like "the favorite of the mighty one of Israel" (so the Jewish Publication Society alternate translation). The plural form given the consonants by the Masoretes may represent an interpretation of the text connecting David with Israel's songs. The other point would seem to have nothing to do with David and the psalms, until viewed in the light of later developments in the tradition. In verses 1–3a, David is clearly portrayed as a person with prophetic capacity. The saying is called an oracle (*ne'um*), a classification used for prophetic sayings. God has spoken first to him, and God's word is what he utters. This happens because the LORD's Spirit uses David to speak. The following poem, in v. 3b–7, is not a psalm. But, as we shall see later, that the psalms are the prophetic words of David will become one of the primary notions of the relation between the two. The idea that David's words might be the word of the LORD about the future messianic king and kingdom begins with this final poem in the narrative of Samuel.

## The Books of Chronicles

In the matter of David and the Psalms, the account of Israel's history in the books of Chronicles shows an interest in one thing alone: David as founder of music and song, the audio component of the Jerusalem cult. So far as we can tell from what is there in the narrative, the circles responsible for the tradition recorded in Chronicles thought of the psalms only as cultic music and saw David's connection with them in terms of the institution and history of public worship in Jerusalem. In their view, Judah's cult rested on two foundations: sacrifice and all else done by the Aaronic priest was based on the ordinance of Moses, but it was by order of David that music was provided (2 Chron. 23:18, see Ezra 3:2, 10).[8]

At the command of David, certain Levites were appointed as singers and musicians to accompany the Ark on the second attempt to bring it to Jerusalem (1 Chron. 15:16–24), and once the Ark was there he designated them "to invoke, to thank, and to praise the LORD, the God of Israel" before the Ark (1 Chron. 16:4). The list of Levites who were appointed varies from text to text, but the role of David never does, and it is reiterated at the end of his career (1 Chron. 23). After that, Chronicles assures the reader that the ordinances of David for music were continued unchanged by Solomon (2 Chron. 8:14), Jehoiada (23:18), Hezekiah (29:25–30), and Josiah (35:15). Throughout the period of the first Temple, David's provisions for music remained in force. According to Ezra 3:10 and Nehemiah 12:25, the continuity of personnel and practice continued into the postexilic era. David is even credited with making the instruments that were used (1 Chron. 23:5; 2 Chron. 7:6; 29:26). He is said also to have designated the liturgical occasions for the use of music (1 Chron. 23:30).

What David contributed to the repertoire of the musical guilds is not clear, and does not seem to be an important issue. Second Chronicles 29:30 says that Hezekiah commanded the Levites to sing praises to the LORD "with the words of David and of Asaph the seer," a note that points to a Davidic and an Asaphite collection. The text knows David as the source of some but not all of the psalms, and suggests that the *ledawid* psalms concerned were viewed as "sayings of David." Second Chronicles 7:6 may say that "David praised by the hand" of the Levites, that is, they were his personal agents, and what they did represented the work of David. Whether this has to do with their office or with what they sang is not clear. The only song quoted in Chronicles is the one sung before the Ark when it was placed in the tabernacle (1 Chron. 16:8–36). It is interesting that this song is a composite of Psalms 105, 96, and 106, all of which have no attribution in the book of Psalms. This could imply either that the Chronicler thought of the psalms as David's or that the issue of their source was unimportant.

Another feature of the Chronicler's portrayal of David is also difficult to assess, though it needs to be noted because of its importance in later notions of David and the psalms. The connection between David and prophecy and song adumbrated in 1 Samuel 23:1–3 becomes much more explicit. The commandment to appoint Levites as musicians is said to have come "from the LORD through his prophets," and David and Gad, the king's seer, and Nathan the prophet are listed as the source of the ordinance (2 Chron. 29:25). The thanking and praising of the Levites appointed by David are called "prophesying" (1 Chron. 25:1–3). The phrase "the words of David and of Asaph the seer" (2 Chron. 29:30) for the praises of the Levites suggests that they are songs regarded as prophetic in character, a collection like "the words of Jeremiah" or "the words of Amos." These all seem to be fragments of a view that connects the institution and performance of Temple music with prophecy, and understands Temple prophecy and cultic praise as generically the same. The possibility of understanding David and his words in the light of the canonical prophets stands at the door.

What is missing in Chronicles in comparison with Samuel is almost as important as what is included. We hear nothing of David the lyrist. The poems of David, the dirge, the song, and the oracle are not included. Of the eleven songs that refer to an occasion in David's story (see in the section below on "the Book of Psalms"), only one can find a context in Chronicles, and that one happens to be an incident of national history rather than Davidic experience (Ps. 60 and 2 Sam. 8:3–8; 10:6–18; 1 Chron. 18:3–11; 19:6–19). The rest of the narrative settings for the psalms are omitted from the account of David's rise and rule. If one only had Chronicles to go with the Psalms, one would find no grounds for using events in David's life as a context for understanding them. All the occasions for lament and penitence are missing. The Chronicler wants David viewed as the founder of Temple music and ordainer of the guilds of musicians, and the psalms as the work of prophetic professionals.

## The Book of Psalms

David appears in the Psalter in three important ways: in the ascription of some psalms to settings in his story, in the simple attribution of many psalms to David, and in what is said about David in the text of a few psalms. This order is probably the reverse of the historical development of the items, but it is the order in which one encounters David in the form of the book.

Psalm 3, the first in the book with a title, is ascribed to David (*ledawid*) and given a setting in a particular occasion of his life. There are ten others whose titles do the same in a formally similar way (34, 51, 52, 54, 56, 57, 59, 60, 63, and 142).[9] Psalm 7 seems to belong to the group, but its status is uncertain because its title does not have the form of the others, and the meaning of the title is unclear. When read as songs sung by David on certain occasions of his career, these psalms cumulatively identify and elaborate one dimension of his story. They all concern situations of need and the deliverance of the LORD as its resolution. They are either prayers for salvation or praise for salvation from trouble or songs of trust on the part of one who must and can live in the face of trouble in reliance on God. In the language of form criticism, they are all individual laments, individual thanksgivings, and songs of confidence.

This common focus on the LORD's salvation as the hope of prayer and the basis of trust points to the importance of the setting given to Psalm 18. Instead of identifying one particular occasion, the title of Psalm 18 is a comprehensive summary composed in a different form from the others. David said this psalm "in the time when the LORD delivered him from the hand of all his enemies, and from the hand of Saul." This title identifies the theme of the entire group, and points to the kind of setting in the story of David in Samuel that goes with the other psalms. Of course, it is also of great importance that Psalm 18 is the only song in the book of Psalms that also appears in the story of David. This makes it the specific literary evidence for how the relationship between the two seems to be understood.

The David in whom those who gave these settings to the twelve psalms are interested is the David whose story is woven out of incidents of trouble, danger from foes within the community and from enemies outside, and finally from his own transgression. But in all, he trod the way of prayer and trust. He was saved. In this pattern of experience, repeated so often in the story when appropriate psalms are related to his crises, he becomes model and guide for those who study the psalms and sing them in worship. The role of the psalms as the key to his life and the truth about it gives the congregation assurance that the practice of life according to these psalms will be the true way for their life. The psalm titles do not grow out of or function in behalf of a historical interest of any kind. They are, rather, hermeneutical ways of relating the psalms to the lives of those who lived in the face of threats from enemies within and without and from their own sin, and who sought to conduct their lives according to the way of David.

Besides the thirteen or twelve psalms with settings in David's story, there are some sixty-one that are simply attributed to David with the phrase *ledawid*. Whatever meaning these simple ascriptions may have had at one time, they are now interpreted in the context of the longer titles that point to David's story. These psalms too can be studied and sung with the same assumptions as the psalms with specific settings. Without the users' having to settle the question of just where they fit in the David story, they offer words to guide thought and worship that hold their users in continuity with David and in relation to David's God. It was some such conviction that gave steady impetus after the canonical Psalter was fixed to the growth of the Davidic claim by the addition of "of David" to other canonical and noncanonical psalms. In the Septuagint, "of David" appears also in the titles of fourteen psalms that do not have the attribution in the Hebrew Bible. When we notice that the attribution was given even to Psalm 137, and that the Greek text has added to Psalm 95 (Masoretic text 96) "of David when the house was built after the captivity," it is apparent that these editors were not thinking historically. Such practices make it very clear that what is at work in the latter history of the *ledawid* attributions is some kind of canonical ordering and defining that proceeds oblivious of any sort of historical or autobiographical concerns.

In this respect, it is important to remember that the Hebrew Psalter provides another significant element as the literary setting of the *ledawid* psalms. A goodly number of the psalms are ascribed to other persons, mostly to the professional guilds of musicians, the Korahites, and Asaphites known from the Chronicler's account. The Psalter does not hold that all psalms are David's, and clearly shows that they are the kind of pieces that are the property of professional groups for the uses of the public cult. Notations in the psalm titles about their use and performance are further evidence that the Psalter does not present the psalms as expressions of David's subjectivity and uniqueness. The full titles imply that the psalms David sang on occasions in his life were precisely the psalms Israel uses in its corporate public worship to express the need, trust, and thanksgiving of many others.

David is specifically named and talked about only comparatively few times in the text of the psalms; the list of those places is Pss. 18:50; 78:70; 89:3, 20, 35, 49; 132:1, 10–11, 17; 144:10 (see 122:5). This short list is, however, of great importance, because it is here that we learn from the Psalter who the David of the titles in the psalms is. The David *in* the psalms is the king of the LORD, the servant of the LORD, the chosen one, the anointed one (messiah), with whom the LORD has made covenant by solemn oath that his dynasty will last forever. The future of all those related to God through David is based on God's sworn promise to David. A very specific sector out of the books of Samuel is reflected in these psalms: the story about Samuel's anointing the shepherd boy (Ps. 78 and 1 Sam. 16), the account of David's introduction of the Ark into Jerusalem (Ps. 132 and 2 Sam. 6), and God's covenant with David (Pss. 89 and 132, and 2 Sam. 7). These are, of course, the stories that give the narrative basis for David's role in the way of the LORD with Israel and the world.

These few texts furnish the inner textual code for reading other psalms in which David is not mentioned. When these titles appear in psalms that do not name David, they furnish the identification for the speaker or subject of the psalm. The "messiah" or "the king" or God's "servant" are textual directions to think of David. When the psalms attributed to David are read in light of what is said in the psalms about him, a messianic construal is cast over the collection. It was inevitable that the psalms would be read in the light of promises of a future Davidic messiah. The role of Psalm 2 as introduction to the canonical book is only one piece of evidence that prophecy has become a rubric in terms of which all the psalms may be read.

## Conclusions

This look at David and the psalms in Samuel, Chronicles, and the book of Psalms uncovers three different presentations of their relationship. Each has features and emphases that are distinctive. But is it also apparent that these distinctive presentations are related in certain ways. They are not connected simply as mere modulations of the same tradition. The texts of one reflect connections with the texts of others, suggesting that they assume a reading that will be made in the light of the others. And, further, it is apparent that the notion of the David of the Psalms, as known to later Jewish and Christian traditions, is not fully and explicitly present in any one of them, though many of the features of the notion can be recognized in each.

These three observations argue that in the Old Testament the notion of the David of the Psalms is an intratextual reality. The notion arises from looking at the texts in terms of certain relations to which the texts themselves guide the reader. It is a product of the Old Testament, not just separate books in it, and in function and effect it is hermeneutical; its usefulness has to do with the interpretation of the text as scripture and in liturgy. It guides understanding in certain directions, restrains it from movement in others, and keeps certain possibilities open. Some of these directions, restraints, and possibilities have been identified here as inner relations between parts of the text came to light. It remains to look at some others with the whole pattern in view.

The intratextual character of the David of the Psalms in the Old Testament is a warning against treating it only or primarily as a historical problem. The question about the historical value of the concerned texts is useful for reconstructing the history of Israel and its tradition. The tentative and thin historical conclusions of critical study of these texts can also be taken as evidence that the historical question does not get at their real character and function. But simply to negate the notion of the David of the Psalms because it is unhistorical, or to eliminate texts like the psalms' titles (as the New English Bible does) because they are secondary, dissolves the intratextual context important for understanding the text and breaks the connection between texts and the church's continuous tradition about them. A postcritical approach to scripture can accommodate historical, literary, and canonical values.

The variety contained in the Old Testament notion of the David of the Psalms is a restraint against a cramping reductionism in their interpretation and use. The variety works against a "nothing but" approach. For instance, the location of the psalms in David's life can lead and has led to an interpretation that makes them so much a part of his individuality and subjectivity that they are removed from common use. The emphasis in Chronicles and in the psalms' titles on the use of the psalms by the community shows that their language transcends the individual to express the typical and traditional. The "I" in the psalms can be a particular person, many people, or the community. On the other hand, form criticism can and sometimes has resulted in such an emphasis on the generic character of the psalms that they are treated as formulaic generalities. The relation to quite specific incidents in David's life furnished by the titles and the story in Samuel demonstrates the true usefulness of the psalms and the purpose of their formulaic character as a religious interpretation of experience that is otherwise chaotic and meaningless.

The relation of the Psalms to David brings out and emphasizes the organizing, unifying subject of the Psalter, the kingdom of God. The subject is explicit in many psalms, of course, and it is easy to show that it is assumed by others. But the Davidic connection directs the reader to think of each psalm and the entire Psalter as an expression of faith in the reign of the LORD as the sphere in which individual and corporate life is lived. It does so because it is quite impossible to separate David from his identity as king chosen to be the regent and agent on earth of God's reign over God's people and the nations of the world. The relation of the Psalms to David makes them a theological interpretation of his office, and the relation of David to the Psalms makes his kingship the context in which their ultimate basis and purpose are clear. To pray and praise through the psalms is to speak the language of those who depend on and trust in the reign of the LORD.

The Davidic relation brings out the prophetic potential in the psalms. David is the king whose throne has an everlasting future based on the promise of God. The songs he sponsored and spoke are to be read in the context of that promise. They are "messianic," not because all of them are about the anointed of Israel, but rather in the sense that they are language to be spoken in the knowledge that God has chosen a messiah and surely keeps God's promises. The Davidic connection makes even the psalms of lament "messianic"; it discloses that suffering borne in trust and hope is a suffering that has a place and role in the reign of God. In turn, David's life becomes an illustration for those who use the psalms of the way in which a life whose hope is in the reign of God is to be lived.

# CHAPTER 10

# "IN A VISION"

## The Portrayal of the Messiah in the Psalms[1]

> No Christ could validate himself as the disclosure of a hidden divine sovereignty over history or as a vindication of the meaningfulness of history, if a Christ were not expected.  —Reinhold Niebuhr[2]

> Jesus is what he is only in the context of Israel's *expectation*. Without the background of this tradition, Jesus would never have become the object of a Christology.  —Wolfhart Pannenberg[3]

The above observations from theologians of the past and present generations affirm the importance of the Old Testament for the career of Jesus and the project of Christology. Both speak of the Old Testament and the traditions of Israel that it transmits in terms of "expectation." The Old Testament texts do not speak about Jesus of Nazareth, at least in readings that will pass muster in our modern intellectual climate. The Jesus of history was not there as reference for these texts. But some of these texts do speak about Yhwh, God of Israel and the world, and of Yhwh's way with Israel and the world, through and in the Messiah of God. In that sense, there is a knowledge of the Messiah/Christ in the Old Testament. The claims of Niebuhr and Pannenberg reflect the confession implied by the biblical canon of the Old Testament and the New Testament that Jesus is not known as Christ apart from the knowledge of the Christ/Messiah of the Old Testament. What the Old Testament says about the Messiah is prolegomena; only from the New Testament do we hear the legomena. The Old Testament provides a description of the person and role of the Christ that is personified by Jesus in an enactment that revises and transcends the description. But it is from the Old Testament that we know the description that is revised and transcended.

When the particular topic of Christology is incarnation as a specific mode of relation between God and Jesus, the movement between the Old Testament and the New Testament witness is narrowed and focused. The Old Testament speaks of the Christ; it does not speak directly of incarnation. The possible connections between such texts as John 1:14 and Proverbs 8 and Philippians 2:5–11 and Isaiah 53 have been explored and discussed thoroughly. What the psalms say, however, about Yhwh's relation to the Messiah of God does have implications for the particular topic, as well as for Christology in general.

## The Approach

What is proposed here is to follow the direction given in the accounts of Jesus' inaugural baptism. Christology as theological work begins with Jesus and the question of the relation between Jesus and God. The baptismal accounts testify that at the beginning of his ministry, a divine word quoted from Psalm 2 was spoken to and about Jesus: "You are my Son" (Mark 1:11 and parallels). The second psalm is the first of a group of psalms in the Psalter that contains the most substantive and coherent testimony to the relation between God and the Messiah of God in the Old Testament, though of course not the only one.

The question of the approach to be taken to these psalms as prolegomena is crucial. They will be read and considered in their genre as scripture. This methodological recognition of their identity in the book of Psalms has important implications that can only be admitted and not argued here. They will not be read under the exclusive constraints of their generic identification in form-critical and cult-functional research as "royal psalms," that is, as texts composed for use in various agenda of rituals for reigning kings of Judah. Their relation to a royal ideology of kingship evident in extrabiblical texts from the general culture of the ancient Near East and their place in the history of religion will not guide the construal. These approaches are valid and have made important contributions to the general understanding of these psalms. In their transmission and shaping and collection as items in the book of Psalms, they, with all the other poetry of the Psalms, "ascended" into another genre. They became scripture, texts whose hermeneutical context is the literary scope of the book in which they stand and the other books of Israel's scriptures. It is in this identity that they "worked" in relation to Jesus and the community in which the New Testament was written. For the purposes of Christology, it is permissible and appropriate to consider them in that identity.

The interest here is to describe some features of the "vision' in these psalms of Yhwh's relation to the "Christ" who speaks and is spoken about in them. The argument is that this vision of the Messiah is as such important material for the work of Christology. The focus will not be on titles and their development in the history of tradition, or on their influence and effect on the historical Jesus or the early Christian communities, the frequent practice in New Testament Christologies. The procedure will be to begin with Psalm 2 in its introductory role and fill out the "vision" of the Messiah from some other psalms whose explicit subject is the Messiah. The exegesis will endeavor to be descriptive, eliciting only what is there in the text, but it will be admittedly selective, guided by the interest of Christology and looking at the potential in the language of the text rather than reductionist.

## Psalm 2

Psalm 2 is the second panel of the introduction to the book of Psalms. It is united to the First Psalm by the inclusion of *'ashre*-sayings which open the First and conclude the Second, and by the repetition of themes from the First (1:6) in the Second (2:12). Together, Psalms 1 and 2 introduce major topics and terms that are woven through the texture of the entire book. The piety represented by these psalms is beset by the problems of the wicked and the nations. The reader is asked to take both psalms as the voice of the speaker, who identifies himself in 2:7 by an identity given him by God. "The son" pronounces the beatitude of Psalm 1 about the wicked and the righteous and discloses the policy of heaven concerning the nations in Psalm 2.

Psalm 2 deals with the problem of the nations governed by kings and rulers. The autonomous exercise of governance by rulers is portrayed as opposition to the sovereignty of Yhwh and his Messiah. The opposition is not related by the text to any particular historical occasion; it is described as a general circumstance and problem for the sovereignty of Yhwh.

The idiom of the psalm is that of kingship, the idiom that is central for the theological vision of the entire book. Yhwh is the universal sovereign throned in the heavens. Any institution of power on earth that does not recognize that sovereignty disrupts and disturbs the reality of the world.

The strategy of Yahweh's rule in answer to the rebellious stratagems of earthly power is the presentation of a king who belongs to the divine sovereignty and represents it. The person and office of this king are wholly the work of Yhwh. He is identified by Yhwh as "my son," an identity that is the result of a divine "begetting" on the day of his presentation. The implication of the text is that this begetting happens through the divine word, "You are my son." This king is located by Yhwh on Zion, the place in the world made holy by the choice of Yhwh. The king belongs to the sphere in worldly space where Yhwh wills to be present as sovereign; he is inseparably related to the presence of the reign of God in the world.

This king is the person to whom God gives the offer and promise to make the nations of the entire world his *naḥalah*, his "assigned portion." In the context of the entire Old Testament, the promise is astonishing in its singularity. Israel and its land are called the *naḥalah* of the LORD as the portion in the world acquired by God's salvation history (e.g., Pss. 28:9; 68:9). Rule over the nations is obviously his to bestow, but "the ends of the earth" are never said to be the *naḥalah* of Yhwh. The nations are to be brought into the reign of God by the Son of God. His rule must correspond to heaven's right and authority. The Messiah will be given power to overcome and claim the powers of earthly rule. But he must ask. His will must be joined to heaven's sovereign will. He must consent to the vocation that sets him in conflict with the rebellious powers of earth for the sake of the reign of God. He must be the Messiah-King-Son in reliance on his identity with the reign of God and the promise of God. From these alone come his power in the world.

In and on the basis of this identity, the Messiah calls the kings and rulers of earth to become servants of the reign of Yhwh. He teaches the nations the fear of the LORD, just as he teaches people obedience to the torah of the LORD (in Ps. 1). To both he offers a better way than the way that offends the divine sovereignty.

The setting of the self-presentation is the sovereignty of Yhwh. The Messiah is identified and described in terms of correspondence to and coherence with the character of the reign of God. It is precisely these dimensions of correspondence and coherence which offer materials for reflection in the work of Christology. These dimensions are what must be looked for in the other psalms that deal with the Messiah.

## Psalm 3

Psalm 3 does not mention the Messiah, but before going on to psalms that do, it is important that we observe a line of reflection opened by its place as the first psalm following the introduction to the book. The superscription of Psalm 3 names the speaker of the introduction, the David of the books of Samuel. We are reminded of the strange and bitter irony that the king identified as son of God once had to flee from Absalom, his own son. Moreover, he was surrounded by many who said there was no salvation for him in God, an even higher irony. He prays for the salvation of God. God's salvation is foundational for his relation to God. The blessing of the people of God depends on and is given through his salvation. The Messiah in the Psalms and in the Old Testament is a quite human figure, vulnerable to the hostility of his own family and the multitudes. His way is the way of prayer and trust. The Third Psalm opens up a line of reflection that is a counterpart to the psalms about the Messiah.

## Psalm 18

Psalm 18 is a psalm of praise for the steadfast love of the LORD manifest in saving help given to the LORD's Messiah, to David and his seed. It is a substantive sequel to the introduction in Psalms 1–2 and Psalm 3, because it testifies that the Messiah who holds to the torah of the LORD and is promised rule over the nations is vindicated in person and vocation when he cries out for the LORD's salvation.

The Messiah, this psalm says, was in the power of his enemies. Their threat was more than mere human hostility. They were instruments of death and Sheol, the elemental powers of opposition to Yhwh as sovereign of the universe, who brought forth the world out of chaos and life out of no life (vv. 4–5). The salvation of the LORD corresponds to the threat. The LORD intervened as the Most High, appearing in the theophany that clothed Yhwh's action against the powers that challenged the divine rule. Cosmic issues were at stake in the Messiah's predicament (vv. 7–15). The salvation of the Messiah is described as the vindication of the reign of God.

The salvation is a vindication of the Messiah, a revelation of God's "delight" in his king (v. 19). The subject of the divine delight is a coherence between the way of the Messiah and the way of the LORD. Both are "perfect" in their ways (vv. 23–30; the Hebrew word is *tamim*, translated "blameless" in v. 23 and "perfect" in v. 30 by NRSV). The Messiah has been perfect in the righteousness of holding to the ways of the LORD known through the LORD's ordinances and statutes. He has been obedient to the will of the divine sovereignty (vv. 20–24). The LORD is perfect in the consistency of his rule and the correspondence between what he promises and does (vv. 25–30). In the salvation of the Messiah, the "perfection" of the faithfulness of the Messiah and the faithfulness of God is known.

It is through the salvation of the LORD that the office and promise of Psalm 2:8–9 is fulfilled. The predicament of the Messiah when he was in the toils of death and cried out to the LORD was answered by a deliverance that established the Messiah as "head of the nations," and brought a people unknown to him into his service (vv. 31–45). The victory given the Messiah in God's salvation brings about the kingdom of God. Hearing about the Messiah as the vindicated of Yhwh compels even foreigners to acknowledge the power of God at work for and in him. God's strength makes the Messiah's way "perfect" (v. 32, again *tamim*, "safe" in NRSV) because it achieves a coherence between his vocation and his work.

The superscription of Psalm 18, and its other literary context at 2 Samuel 22, connect it with all David's escapes from Saul and all his battles with the enemies of Israel. The psalm stands in that connection as a theological interpretation of David's career as servant of the LORD. There was, says the superscription, a "day when the LORD delivered him from the hand of all his enemies." Deliverance from all enemies is an eschatological hope of the people of God. This hope was realized one day in David's career as a proleptic manifestation of what God intends to accomplish through David's seed for the servants of the LORD.

## Psalm 72

Psalm 72 is a prayer for the king. From beginning to end the psalm is intercession on the king's behalf. The agenda of the intercession covers all the endowments and accomplishments that belong to the royal rule in its fullness and perfection. As the prayer proceeds through its agenda, it becomes apparent that what God is asked to enable the king to do is that which the psalms elsewhere attribute to the work of the divine sovereignty. The king himself is to be the medium and source of righteousness, well-being (shalom), victory, and abundance. He is to exercise universal rule over all kings and nations. His name should endure forever, and the nations bless themselves by that name as God's promise to Abraham is kept through him (compare v. 17 and Gen. 12:1–3). Especially, the king is to be the officer of the LORD's merciful justice, which saves the lives of the lowly and helpless when they cry to him (vv. 2, 4, 12–14). The correlation between the role and way of the LORD and that of the king for whom the prayer is made is unmistakable. The prayer envisions and prays for a king who will make it possible for the people of God and the nations of the world to live in the kingdom of God. This, the prayer confesses, all depends on the promise and power of the divine judgments and righteousness in the person of the king.

The prayer is made, says its opening line, for a king who is a king's son. The superscription connects the prayer with Solomon, and the colophon at the conclusion (v. 20) says the psalm is the last in the sequence of David's prayers before the psalms of Asaph begin. Superscription and colophon taken together ask that the prayer be read as David's intercession for his seed and successor, a prayer that the vocation of God's king be realized in his son. In the light of the story of Solomon, it is evident how incompletely the vocation materialized in him. The prayer has a dimension and reach that transcend Solomon and all the kings of Judah. Within the Old Testament, it prays for what is not yet—a king whose person and practice bring the people of God and the nations of the earth into the time of the reign of God.

## Psalm 89

Psalm 89 is a lament over the rejected Messiah. It is the opposite of Psalm 18 and the contradiction of Psalm 2. It sets forth in anguish an unbearable, inscrutable mystery. The Messiah suffers the wrath of his father and his God, the rock of his salvation. The chosen one is now the rejected one. That reversal is the plot of the psalm and the problem for which it sees no resolution. In its long course, it elaborates more fully than anywhere else the correspondence and coherence between the sovereignty of God and the person of the Messiah, because the theological fact of that relationship is the burden of its dilemma. The theme of the lament is God's sworn covenant to establish the rule of David's house forever (vv. 3–4, 28–29, 36–37). The fate of the Messiah has rendered the steadfast love and faithfulness of God invisible.

The LORD reigns supreme in the heavens, incomparable among all the heavenly powers, who only form the council of holy ones around the heavenly throne (vv. 6–8). Correspondingly, according to God's promise, God's king is to be the highest of all the kings of earth (v. 27). The LORD is the cosmic warrior who defeated the powers of chaos and founded the earth and all that is in it (vv. 9–12). The Messiah is a warrior chosen from among the people of God and given power over the unruly forces of history. "Seas and river," the symbols of chaos, will be ordered by his rule (vv. 19–25). Just as the LORD has firmly established his rule over the universe forever, he will establish forever the rule of the Messiah (vv. 2, 28–29).

The point of this carefully drawn parallel between the kingship of God and that of David claims that the latter is integral to the former. The Messiah's rule actualizes in the world what is reality in heaven and cosmos. David's kingship is the agency through which the LORD's rule is extended from heaven to earth, and the divine dominion over cosmic chaos is expanded to include historical disorder. Just as sun and moon are in the heavens, so David's line will be the enduring witness on earth to the reign of the LORD.

The time of the psalm, the "but now" of verse 38, is a time for the people of God that stands in utter contradiction to the sworn covenant with David. The defeat, humiliation, deposition, and even death (possibly the inference of v. 45) of Yhwh's anointed constitute God's renunciation of the covenant. Divine wrath inexplicably prevails. The steadfast love of God and the righteousness of God are put in question. If the earthly correspondent to the heavenly rule is vanquished and vanishes, what of the heavenly rule itself? That is the overwhelming enigma for which the psalm knows no resolution.

## Psalm 110

Psalm 89, with its shattering quandary, concludes Book III of the Psalter. It would seem to set closure on the vision of the anointed king of God and the question of his relation to God. But twice more a voice is heard filling out the vision and addressing the question. In Psalm 110 the voice is that of the LORD, apparently speaking through a prophet. The king is invited to sit at the right hand of the LORD—the place closest to a monarch, the place that identifies a regent with the one whose rule he shares and serves. Another sworn promise of God is given the regent. He is made a priest according to the order of Melchizedek—forever. The Messiah is to be a king whose rule provides a priestly ministry. God himself will be at the right hand of the regent on his right hand, and will establish his reign. His people will respond willingly. The horizon of the psalm is the time when the divine warrior has finally and completely defeated and subjected all the hostile powers of earth to the Messiah, and the promise of Psalm 2 is kept. Until that time the Messiah is at God's right hand, exercising the priesthood of one whose rule mediates between the world and its sovereign. The horizon of the session at the right hand and the royal priesthood is the horizon of history.

## Psalm 132

In Psalm 132, the voice is the voice of pilgrims going up to Zion. They speak about the relation between David and Zion and the LORD and hope. The psalm begins as a prayer (vv. 1–10) and concludes with a recitation of the promises of the LORD (vv. 11–18). The psalm beseeches the LORD to remember all the afflictions of David which he endured in finding a dwelling place for the LORD. The establishment of Jerusalem as Zion, the place of the LORD's presence, is viewed as the climax and destiny of David's life. All his troubles were self-denials (vv. 3–5) to provide the place of the Presence, where priests are clothed in righteousness and the faithful shout with joy. The pilgrims appeal to the LORD to be present at the place for the sake of David, his Messiah, whose suffering was the human means of its establishment.

The prayer is grounded in the citation of two divine decrees. The first is the LORD's sworn and certain oath that David's kingship would continue in his descendants if they keep the requirements of the covenant. The prayer looks for a Messiah whose career is covenant-true. The Messiah must actualize the obedience and faithfulness required by the divine sovereignty over the people of the LORD. The second is the LORD's election of Zion as the place of his salvific presence. The afflictions of David served and fulfilled the divine purpose. Place and person are united by the confluence of divine will and human service. Because the two are inseparable in the LORD's reign over earth, the LORD will there bring forth "a horn for David . . . a lamp for my messiah." The place and the person presented in Psalm 2 as the institution of heaven's reign in the world are here the subjects of hope.

## Conclusion

These, then, are some of the principal features of the vision of the relation between the Messiah and God in the Psalms. It is, of course, an Old Testament vision. It is articulated in the vocabulary of its time and in the idiom of the protagonists in whom it was given human expression. But its royal, political, military language is not irrelevant so long as the great metaphor of the reign of God is useful to the thinking of faith seeking understanding. The language is not abandoned in the New Testament, but rather redefined and informed by the subject that becomes its content here. The New Testament points to another dimension of the Psalms, which is only mentioned in this review because of its concentration on texts that deal with the anointed king of God. That other dimension appears in the sequence initiated by Psalm 3 and comes to fullest expression in Psalms 22, 31, and 69.

It portrays one whose forsakenness and deliverance become, mysteriously, the ground of faith in the reign of God. But that is all the subject of another study.

It serves the purpose of the vision best if a systematic and conceptual condensation is not attempted as a conclusion. Such an abstraction easily becomes itself the subject of thought. The vision is best considered in attempted descriptions that are responses to particular texts and their literary and canonical connections. The vision is never fully in focus, never complete in some logical form. In each text it is a refraction of what the text speaks about.

The vision brings perspective and depth to the New Testament witness to Jesus. When Jesus comes into Galilee announcing that the kingdom of God has drawn near because he is there (Mark 1:15), the vision is in the background. When Jesus at the end of Matthew's Gospel tells his disciples, "All authority in heaven and on earth has been given to me. Go therefore, make disciples of the nations" (Matt. 28:16–20), the vision is in the background. When Paul writes the Corinthian church about the end, when Christ hands over the kingdom to God the Father after he has destroyed every ruler and authority and power (1 Cor. 15:24), the vision is in the background. The contribution of the vision to Christology is the perspective and depth disclosed when connections like these are made. In their light, do we claim too much if we confess that the reign of God was "incarnate" in Jesus?

# CHAPTER 11

# "YOU ARE MY SON"
## An Interpretation of Psalm 2

Every time we Christians confess our faith using the ancient creeds we say, "I believe in Jesus Christ, God's only Son, our Lord." When we read the Gospels we hear that Jesus of Nazareth was called Christ/Messiah, Lord, King, Son of God. Creed and Gospels seem to assume that all those titles go together—but they do not ever explain how this is so or what they mean.

Psalm 2 is an Old Testament text that was spoken over Jesus at his baptism (Matt. 3:17 and parallels), in which all the titles occur (King, Messiah, Son of God) and in which someone is called "son of God."

I want to use Psalm 2 as a door opening on the interpretive history that lies behind calling Jesus "Son of God," Messiah, King.

Here is my procedure:

1. A look at the psalm, a brief exposition
2. A look through the psalm at the ancient Near Eastern cultural and religious history to which it is related
3. An account of Israel's prophetic revision of the psalm's subject
4. A discussion of the significance of this history for Jesus of Nazareth
5. Some concluding reflections on the "Word" in the psalm

Here is the thesis:

To call Jesus "Son of God" is to understand him as the resolution and solution to humanity's ancient and continuing quest for one who would have and use power to make it possible for people:
  to live in the kingdom of God
  to experience power as blessing
  to experience peace, welfare, and justice as the circumstance of life

— I —

As poetry, the psalm has a striking and dramatic aesthetic of composition. There are four equal stanzas, each of which plays its role in creating what the

108

psalm wants us to see and hear, and therefore to know. Verses 1 and 3 look out over the political history of the world with a question, "Why do the nations conspire, and the peoples plot in vain?" The question gathers up the entire scene of governments and rulers, grasping and consolidating power, working out their destiny in terms of force; and it interprets the machinations of the whole thing theologically as rebellion against the Lord and his Anointed.

The second strophe, verses 4 through 6, looks from earth to heaven, and sees there the vision of the King who is throned over all the powers of this earth and portrays his reaction. The portrayal is couched in anthropomorphisms. The "laughter" of God at the earthly, frantic plotting is the symbol for his invulnerable sovereignty. The "wrath" of God is the Old Testament theological language for his invincible purpose to maintain sovereignty. The stanza ends with a divine word that states the strategy of God against the powers of this earth: "I have set my king on Zion, my holy hill."

In verses 7 through 9, an unidentified speaker is heard. The person who takes up the word can only be the king of verse 6. He recites the decree of the king in heaven, and it has two parts. The first is his designation as the son of God. God has "begotten" him on the very day he speaks. The language is that of the legal adoption procedure of the ancient Near East. The second part of the decree is a promise. The nations are to be his heritage as son. He will wield power over them. It is the will of the heavenly King that the rebellious nations of earth should end up in the power of the one designated his son.

The final stanza, verses 10 through 12, is an exhortation, an address to the kings of earth. It is the *applicatio* of all that has gone before. The exhortation is a summons to the kings and the rulers to submit to the LORD as king. And one notes in the form of this summons that it is not the son to whom the nations are to bow, but heaven's rule. The son is an instrument of that sovereignty. The exhortation concludes with a threat and a promise. Those who resist the strategy of heaven will perish and those who take refuge in the kingdom of God are blessed.

Now there is no question about the theme of this remarkable poem. If we apply the principle of repetition, the answer is obvious. The nations and their kings appear in every one of the four stanzas. The psalm is consummately concerned with the world of politics and history, the peoples and their governments. The purpose of the psalm is clear in the progress of thought through the parts. It sets forth the relation between the kingdom of heaven and the kingdoms of earth, a relation at whose focus stands the figure called Messiah and "son." Through that figure, whose royalty is the creation of the divine reign, God deals with the powers of the earth.

But it is just this clarity of theme and purpose which sharpens the central question about the psalm. Who is the one named "son of God"? We must not think with the New Testament too quickly here. We know the answer, but

we do not know what the answer means unless we understand the significance of the psalm as an Old Testament witness. When Jesus is called Son of
God, it means he enters into a role prepared both by the general experience of
humanity and by the prophetic insight that belongs to Israel. It is only from
texts like Psalm 2 that we can know into what office he enters and what
expectations he fulfills in appearing as Son of God.

— II —

In its Old Testament context, to what, to whom does the title "son of
God" point? Recognizing what kind of text Psalm 2 is and how it was used in
Israel provides a first partial answer. It belongs to a group of ten or more
psalms that are classified as royal psalms (the list includes Pss. 18; 20; 21; 45;
72; 89; 110). The basic characteristic that holds them together is that they all
have as their central subject a living, reigning king of Judah. In occasion and
function, these psalms are quite varied. The group includes corporate
petitions for the king, prayers by him and for him before and after battle, a
song for a royal wedding, and pieces belonging to the ritual of his accession to
office. In all this variety, they serve one purpose. They speak of the place the
office of the king had in the faith of Israel. They witness that the king had a
focal role in Israel's status, welfare, and destiny under God.

Now in this function Psalm 2, and the rest of the royal psalms, are part of a
much wider literature of a similar kind. Such prayers, songs, and rituals appear
in the known literature of the nations of the ancient Near East, from the Nile
to the Mesopotamian area. There are many kinds of similarities between the
royal literature of other peoples and the royal psalms of Israel: expressions,
form, and function. So royal psalms do have a context that is broader than
Israel and its specific faith. And the implication is clear. Only by reading them
within this broader context will they be fully understood. And, in particular, it
is only in this way that we can learn the full import of the question "To whom
does the title 'son of God' refer?" What does it mean that it is used of a quite
human political, mortal figure?

To recognize this—and to read the psalms in this broader context—is not
a disadvantage, a concession to be made fearfully, defensively. Scripture
serves its holy purpose, not only in its distinction from the religious literature
and cultures of others. It serves not only in its uniqueness, but as well in its
continuities, in the way it draws the needs, aspirations, and experiences of all
humanity into the sphere of the LORD's plan and purpose. There are
advantages to us in our work of apprehending the revelation of the LORD
when we read in this broader context.

First and perhaps least important, we can understand in this way why
certain language in the psalm that seems harsh and bizarre is used, and how it

is to be understood. Take verse 9, for instance. Part of the promise to the son that he will possess the nations of the earth says: "You shall break them with a rod of iron, and dash them in pieces like a potter's vessel." Read literally, those two lines seem cruel and pointless. They smack of an insane tyranny that possesses only to destroy. But in its original sphere of use, these words were not meant in that way at all. Behind them is a ritual, known particularly from the ceremonies of Egypt as part of the procedures of installing a king. The names of the nations over which he claimed sovereignty would be written on clay tablets, and in a symbolical ritual the king would smash those tablets with his scepter. Translated, this dramatic ritual language simply means, "You shall claim and rule them with a power they cannot resist."

Take verses 11–12, with their strange exhortation, "Serve the LORD with fear, with trembling kiss his feet." Numerous examples from the art of Bronze and Iron Age cultures show representatives of subject people at the time of the accession of a king, prostrating themselves before him, touching their foreheads to the royal foot. Once again, we are dealing with a ritual of the recognition of the sovereignty of a great king by vassal peoples. The ritual is simply an enactment of the confession, "We are your servants," which is precisely the point of the exhortation.

Such illuminations of the language of the text show us that in the royal psalms Israel has taken up and entered into a sphere of expression common to the social history of its world and age. It was language prepared by the general human history to speak about what Israel in its inspiration wanted and had to speak about—the question of power on earth and its relation to God.

Second, by comparison with the royal traditions of other peoples, we can be more certain of what is happening in the psalm, of the transaction that its language represents. Analogies in the literature of Mesopotamia and especially of Egypt make it clear that the psalm belongs to one moment in the ritual in the inauguration of a king. The accession usually consisted of two main acts. The king was crowned in the sanctuary, where he received the royal record that contained the actual commission to rule given by the deity and, in addition, the new king's throne name—in a word, his legitimation as a ruler commissioned by God. After he had been crowned, he was then conducted to his palace, where he ascended his throne and in a more or less threatening way announced in a general proclamation the start of his rule. Psalm 2 almost certainly has its place here. The king who reads the psalm is reporting the commission to rule given him in the sanctuary and directing an ultimatum to the nations.

The significance of the somewhat mysterious question that opens the psalm in verses 1 and 2 comes into view. At the time of the change of the rulers, all the vassals would use the shift as an opportunity to rebel. The accession of a new king of the realm was then, by custom and ritual, the occasion for asserting the authority of the king's office anew, for construing any moves toward independence as rebellion.

Incidentally, when you think about Judah's situation, about the actuality of the political situation in which Psalm 2 was used, then the incredible boldness in the procedure is astonishing. Judah was a county-sized kingdom and Jerusalem was a county-seat capital. The language of Psalm 2 might sound a bit more credible in the capitals of the great empires of the ancient world, but in Jerusalem, viewed in the cold eye of historical reality, it rises to the height of ridiculousness. But behind this boldness is a confidence that Yahweh alone is God. The king whom he selects, alone among those for whom this language is used in the ancient world, is the one of whom all this can be said. And it was said, against all appearances, in unbearable tension, over and over in Judah.

Third, it is in the context of the thought-world of other peoples that we can see the crucial importance for human existence of the event in which one is named "son of God." The designation of a king had its background in an ancient process as old as social order itself. Wherever and whenever, in the deep history of the ancient Near East, a group of human beings felt compelled to recognize one above others, was led by need to deal with the question of power and the quest for power within their social group and in competition with others, this process was at work. The leader became the agent of power and the source of power. In the society of the ancient Near East known to us, it was believed that power flowed from the deity to the people through the king. He, the king, was the provider of the three basic needs of society: of security against enemies—he was the leader in warfare; of justice and order—he was the judge par excellence; of well-being—the integrity of his relation to the gods was the channel of blessings.

That such a view of the king was held in Judah is evident from another of the royal psalms, Psalm 72, where the congregation itemizes precisely these three expectations of the king in prayer in his behalf. "May he judge thy people with righteousness and the poor with justice. Let the mountains bear prosperity for the people and the hills, in righteousness. . . . May his foes bow down before him and his enemies lick the dust."

When the king was named "son of God," the title was a confession of faith that the king was the representative and agent of the deity in such unity and coherence that only the term "son" could display the correspondence and claims between the two. How the reality was created to which the title pointed was conceived in a variety of ways in the general culture. But common to all of them was the belief that the king was a divine instrument of life for those he ruled.

So when the psalm was recited by a Davidide in Jerusalem, it was a proclamation that the LORD had chosen to provide life through the office in which the Davidide was installed. The inauguration of his reign created the opportunity for blessing or perishing, depending on the response to the announcement of his kingship. He was there as a chance for the world to live in the reign of God, to find refuge and not perish.

The Second Psalm gathers all this background of social and religious experience into Israel's theology. And it can address itself to all the kings and nations of earth precisely because it speaks their language, knows their need, brings to a penultimate climax their search.

— III —

But just as surely as the psalm in the Old Testament context is affected by the general understanding of kingship in its culture, it stands over against it in sharp distinction. The psalm is not just one more case of ancient Near Eastern royal ideology. Rather, it represents the movement in which the cultural history of kingship is being translated into the history of the coming of the Messiah. And it claims that it is in the kingship of Judah that the true God is working out the true response to the question about and the quest for the power that saves.

One way to identify and describe the uniqueness of the kingship about which Psalm 2 speaks is to say that it has a prophetic origin, a prophetic history, and a prophetic destiny. The kingly office in view in the Second Psalm had its essential definition in the promissory covenant the LORD made with David through Nathan the prophet. When the LORD says in verse 6, "I have set my king on Zion, my holy hill," the declaration points to a quite specific and unique event in Israel's history. The classic text for that event, of course, is 2 Samuel 7. There David is planning to build a house for the LORD. Nathan receives word from the LORD that David is not to build a house (that is, a temple) for the LORD. Instead, the LORD will build a house (that is, a dynasty) for David. In this play on words, and in the reversal in that message, lies something fundamental about Old Testament kingship. It was customary in the ancient days for kings to build temples for their patron deity. The temple and its cult were, in fact, an expression of the glory and policy of the human king. The prophetic words shut the door on that course to David. Instead, Yahweh would build David a house, a succession of heirs to come after him. The Davidic kingship must always be the expression of the power of Yahweh's promise and always be subordinate to its fulfillment. The permanence of that kingship would be the permanence of the promise. Wherever "son of God" was said over a Davidide in the long history of Judah, it meant that Yahweh was keeping his covenant. The kingship was wholly subsumed to the powerful purpose of God. It was meant to have no policy or purpose beyond those which belonged to the LORD and which were

announced by the prophets. That is why the psalm concludes, not with a call
to do obeisance to the king, but with a summons to the world to find in the
Davidic king the occasion to acclaim the kingdom of Yahweh.

Old Testament kingship had a prophetic history from its beginning until
its end in the sixth and fifth centuries. From David himself, down to the end
of his line in the exile and the obscure revival around Zerubbabel during the
restoration, prophets accompanied the long and tortured career of Old
Testament kingship. Just as it began with a prophetic word, it was pursued
and beset by prophets who served as messengers of the king of heaven to his
regent and representative in Jerusalem. The record of the sustained encounter between kings and prophets is written in the books of Kings and in the
books of the prophets. It is, of course, a record of judgment. The prophetic
voices made it clear that there was an unbearable contradiction between the
royal office borne by David's successors and the way they used its authority
and privilege. They were both bearers and betrayers of the calling to make it
possible for their subjects to live in the reign of God. The office sustained by
the promise endured, but its incumbents were swept away in the ongoing
crisis worked by the One whose sole purpose is his own coming kingdom.

It was in the contradiction in its career that the prophetic destiny of Old
Testament kingship appeared. Alongside the royal psalms and their word
about the divine purpose for Judah's kings, there began to be heard the
prophecy of one yet to come.

> There shall come forth a shoot from the stump of Jesse,
>     and a branch shall grow out of his roots.
> And the Spirit of the LORD shall rest upon him. . . .
> He shall not judge by what his eyes see
>     or decide by what his ears hear,
> but with righteousness he shall judge the poor,
>     and decide with equity for the meek of the earth. . . .
> The wolf shall dwell with the lamb
>     and the leopard shall lie down with the kid. . . .
> They shall not hurt or destroy
>     in all my holy mountain:
> for the earth shall be full of the knowledge of the LORD
>     as the waters cover the sea.
>                                         (Isa. 11:1–9)

There began to be speech about "the Messiah" in the broadest sense of
that term. Messianic prophecy means that the promise endured where its
instruments failed. Under the powerful influence of that prophecy, the royal
psalms themselves came to be read as hope for "the One who comes." The
kings had disappeared, but the purpose of God to designate one through

whom peace, justice, and blessing were created entered into prophecy. So within the Old Testament context itself, Psalm 2 became messianic prophecy. The inauguration it described awaited a candidate. The title "Son of God" hung in the air, because there was no specific historical human person to whom it could be given.

— IV —

When Jesus of Nazareth was baptized by John, the title was given for a final time. The Gospels tell us that heaven said to him and of him "Son of God." With that designation, the background of the psalm in world history and its redefinition in prophetic history were brought to bear on him. In him, the promise to David is kept and the covenant of God maintained in force. His life unfolds in such congruence with the purpose of God that there is no disparity between the will of God and the way of his anointed. The whole human history of making kings in hope of finding the one among many whose person unites, saves, and blesses, instead of alienating, betraying, and exploiting, comes to rest in him. He is a human being whose life makes it possible for the rest to live in the reign of God. From him the rest of us can receive justice, peace, and wholeness. All this is claimed and announced when the Gospel records that he began his work under the sign of the Second Psalm.

The entire life of Jesus, from baptism to crucifixion, was his accession, his public presentation to the nations and their rulers, as the Messiah. This means that the psalm has a new setting in the Gospel. It is heard now, not in a palace in the midst of royal ritual, but in a ritual of repentance-baptism in which Messiah takes on his career the rubric, "Not my will, but thine." This setting for his accession is the first sign that the quest for power as the hope of salvation will receive a radically different answer in his execution of office. He will use no other power than the power of justice, faithfulness, and love. He invests and exhausts himself in them in such a way as to make their power visible in his weakness. He teaches that power separated from them becomes mere force: it destroys; it is demonic. The reign of God is found only in willing, thankful acceptance of the justice, faithfulness, and love revealed and offered in Jesus.

— V —

This, then, is the account of the most crucial theme in the long and complex story of the human race. It is the narrative plot of humanity's search for One who would have and use power to make it possible for humans to live in the reign of God—to experience power as blessing, to find security, justice, and peace.

    a. The ancient world sought it from rulers who had absolute power and were called sometimes "Son of God" as a title of their office to be representative and agent of a deity.

    b. Israel redeemed that hope by relating it to the true God.

    c. The prophets reformed that hope by relating it to a future Messiah who would be truly the agent of the true God.

    d. Jesus transformed that hope by relating it to the power of grace and love enacted in his life, death, and resurrection.

When Jesus, at the end of Matthew's Gospel, says to the disciples, "All power is given me in heaven and on earth. Go, therefore, teach and baptize the nations"—when Jesus says that, we are hearing the fulfillment of Psalm 2.

All who today make the confession "Jesus is the Son of God" continue that story. They/you/we are the participants at the point where the plot is acted out in the present. The history makes clear the enormous significance of the confession. For those who believe that Jesus is the Son of God, there are consequences that change the way life is viewed and lived.

1. Government is desacralized. If Jesus is the agent of God's reign, no politics has a divine right and role. The human vesting and organization of power is pragmatic, temporary, provisional. Fanatic patriotism, which places country or state above all else, is made a heresy. Ideologies of the absolute state, whether of the right or the left, are denied.

2. To have Jesus as the Messiah of God means that he alone makes it possible for us to live in the kingdom of God—now, and in the world to come. No revolutionary reordering of society, no economic system, can, in fact, bring in the kingdom. In *this life* we receive the blessing of God's reign by faith as spiritual gifts through the Christ: justice in the form of justification by grace, well-being in the form of salvation, and peace in the form of reconciliation with God. And it is because of these gifts and by the strength of these gifts that we work for human justice, prosperity, and peace in society and in the world.

3. God makes the claims of his rule on people, societies, and nations through the crucified and risen Christ. God's power to save is manifested through the Spirit of the risen Lord. God does not bring people into his kingdom by power used as force. And all use of force, all trust in force as a way to justice, well-being, and peace, is suspect.

4. If psalm and Gospel are right—if God lays claim on the nations through the Son, and Jesus is the Son—if that is true, then Jesus is the one offer of God to human history. There is no other divine plan, no other strategy of heaven, to meet our needs and to save us from the consequences of human folly and wickedness. There is only this Jesus.

# PART 5

# The Psalms as Book and Scripture

Good and upright is the LORD;
   therefore he instructs sinners in the way.
He leads the humble in what is right,
   and teaches the humble his way.
                              —Psalm 25:8–9

# CHAPTER 12

# GOING BY THE BOOK
## The Psalter as a Guide to Reading Psalms

Psalms are customarily read and used one by one. Each is known and dealt with on its own. They are read and sung and prayed and studied as individual literary units. The book is simply the source from which each is taken, the literary location where they are found. The book is treated as an anthology, a collection that contains the psalms. The book rarely comes into consideration in liturgical use or devotional reading. It is not itself the object of study in the way that the books of Exodus and Samuel and Luke are.

Modern critical study of the psalms has not been much concerned with the book as a literary unit. The primary interest has been in the origin of the psalms and in their place in Israel's religious life. It moved behind the book, back into periods when the book did not exist. Psalms criticism has sought for historical and social and cultic contexts in which to understand the meaning and purpose of the psalms. Where the book was a topic of investigation, the plan has been to reconstruct its growth. The focus has not been on the literary reality of the book and what its character might mean for understanding and interpreting the psalms that compose it.

In recent years, however, there has been an increased interest in the book itself.[1] Questions that put the book in focus as a literary reality are the subject of discussion and investigation. How may the shape and character of the book be described? What can be said about its purpose on the basis of its final form and content? What does its literary character mean for understanding and interpreting the psalms of which it is composed? There are a number of reasons for this shift to focus on the book.

First, this interest in the book is part of a broad movement in biblical studies that has been building for some time. In the broad development of criticism, "the time of the book" has come. There is a new appreciation of the biblical books as important realities that transcend their parts and their past. There is more to a book than how it came to be, so there is more to learn about a book than genetic explanations. The narrative books of New and Old

119

Testaments were the initial focus of interest. But the books of the prophets, and now the Psalms, have become subjects of study.

Second, there is a growing recognition that the psalms in the book are not simply the psalms of their origin in various settings in Israel's religious life. They have been revised and reread in the process of reuse and preservation. They are located in a new and final context of a book of scripture with an understanding of their language and purpose that is not identical with their meaning in Israel's cult. This final literary context is a setting that calls for study in its own right, along with historical and cultic settings.

Third, it is apparent that the psalms as understood in the context of the book are closer to and in most direct continuity with their use in the New Testament and in the liturgy and theology of the church.

## — II —

The question about the Psalms as a book is a question about literary features that organize and unify the whole and its contents. What is there in the text that transcends the parts to make it more than mere collection? How does its shape, its arrangement and sequence, supply a context for reading the psalms in the book? The features generally recognized can be divided into those that concern the collection as a whole and those that involve sequences or groupings within the whole.

Features that concern the whole are as follows.

1. The collection is divided into five parts, or "books" as they have come to be named. They are identified by "doxologies" that conclude the last psalm in the first four books (41:13; 72:18–19; 89:52; 106:48). The five books are, thus, Psalms 1—41, 42—72, 73—89, 90—106, 107—150. Psalm 150 seems to serve as the concluding doxology for Book V and the entire Psalter.

2. Psalms 1 and 2 form an introduction to the whole. They are held together by the "Happy are/is . . ." form of the sayings that constitute brackets around the two. Each contains a distinctive topic and set of themes that recur throughout the book.

3. Psalms 146—150 form the conclusion of the book. They are a block of psalms that begin and end with "Praise the LORD" (translation of "Hallelujah"). All five praise the LORD for his mighty deeds as sovereign of the world and God of his people. The themes of this praise summarize and repeat the characterizations of the LORD throughout the Psalter.

4. There are large groupings of psalms established by the reference to persons in the superscriptions that head these psalms. Psalms 3—41 and 51—72, as well as 108—110 and 138—145, are connected with David. The other groups are the psalms connected to the Korahites (42—49 and 84—89) and to Asaph (73—83). The first David group makes up Book I, while Book II is composed of Korahite and Davidic psalms, with the Asaphite fifty between

them. Book III is composed of Asaphite and Korahite psalms. Book V has blocks of the David psalms near its beginning and end. The effect is to give the book as a whole a Davidic cast, with the second block of David psalms folded into concentric rings of Korahite and Asaph psalms.

5. The superscriptions of many of the psalms include identifications and notes connected with musical performance. They are named variously "a psalm" or "a song" or "a *shiggaion*" or "according to the *Gittith*," and so on. Many are noted as belonging in some way "to the leader," an office or function connected with the music of the Temple in Jerusalem.

Along with such features which give shape to the book as a whole, other patterns of arrangement have been noted that concern two or more psalms as a grouping within the larger framework. (1) Sequences are created by the repetition of a phrase or catchword from a psalm in the psalm that follows. Psalms 134 and 135 both open with a summons to praise the LORD addressed to "the servants of the LORD who stand in the courts of the LORD!" (2) Psalms appear sometimes as a complementary pair matched by various devices. Psalms 103 and 104 are the only psalms that employ the self-invocation, "Bless the LORD, O my soul." The topic of the first is God as savior, who forgives sinners, and of the second is God as creator, who sustains all life. Together they provide a meditation on the two typical works of the LORD. (3) There are clusters of psalms that are grouped by content. Psalms 90 through 100 feature the theme and topic of the reign of the LORD and establish it as a primary motif at the beginning of Book IV.

Awareness of these literary features of the Psalter is of course nothing new. Most of them are duly listed in every critical introduction to the Psalms. But in such contexts, these features are used as evidence for the formation of the book. How do they help us understand the process and phrases of the writing, transmission, and collection of psalms on the way to the creation of the Psalter? Here the question is about their significance as guides to reading and understanding the book of Psalms and the psalms as part of the book. The answer to that question could, of course, demand and involve a commentary on the entire book.[2] In a shorter study, one can simply cite illustrations of what "going by the book" might mean. The following are among the more obvious and important possibilities.

— III —

Let us begin at the beginning. Beginnings are important in a book, and the First Psalm as half of the book's two-part introduction tells the reader some important things about the book.

First, it identifies the function of the book. The book is torah of the Lord.[3] Torah means instruction, teaching, direction that can be given in various literary forms. The psalms provide torah that can be learned by study and meditation. It is scripture where one learns about God and God's way with the world. This identification concerns the comprehensive use of the psalms gathered into the book. It does not deny that many are written to function as prayers and hymns of praise. In the book, the hymns and prayers are to be read as torah of the LORD.

The fivefold division of the book continues the identification. It gives the book a form that corresponds to the five books of the Mosaic Torah. The Psalter is a "Davidic Torah," which corresponds to and responds to the first one. The doxologies at the end of each book bless the LORD God and thereby serve as literary indications that what is important about the psalms in each book is the witness given to the works and way of the LORD. The prayers and hymns and poems of instruction are to be read because they speak of God.

Second, the introductory psalm poses a topic that is constant and crucial in the book, the opposition between the righteous and the wicked. The expression and meaning of that opposition will be dealt with in different and dialectical ways in the following psalms. The antonyms will be the nucleus of a word-field of synonyms and related vocabulary. But the First Psalm lays down principles basic to every particular. Life is at stake. The sovereignty of the LORD is at issue. The reader is duly instructed by the First Psalm to attend the topic in its constant recurrence as a constitutive term of the book.

The Second Psalm, as the other half of the book's introduction, serves corresponding and complementary functions. One notes that the second part does not depart from the style of instruction, but begins with a didactic question and ends with an exhortation and beatitude.

Here also a topic is identified that is central and recurrent in the book as a whole: the kingship of the LORD.[4] The LORD appears as one who reigns. His reign in the work is represented by a place and a person. The place is Zion. The person is his chosen king. Zion as city of God and king as the LORD's anointed will themselves be the subject of many particular psalms. What happens to and through them involves the reign of the LORD. And it is this theme of the reign of God that is the integrating center of the theology of the entire book. All else is in one way or another connected to and dependent on this divine sovereignty.

Here too a thematic opposition is stated, the contrast between the reign of the LORD and the nations and peoples and their kings and rulers. The autonomy of the individual in the presence of the LORD's torah and the autonomy of social groups and their leaders in the presence of the LORD's reign are together and in interrelated ways the poles of the problematics of the Psalter. The torah of the LORD is the answer to the first, and the anointed king is presented in the Second Psalm as God's response to the second.

The two psalms together call for a piety composed of obedience and trust that is fostered by the entire book. Delight in the torah and taking refuge in the LORD constitute the faith nurtured by the psalms. The psalms offer a "way" and a "refuge" in the midst of the wickedness and power of this world.

— IV —

The two introductory psalms are not identified with an author or speaker. They have a purely literary role in the framework of the book. The Third Psalm, however, is attributed to David; he is identified as the "I" whose voice is heard in most of the psalms. The Third Psalm opens the successive blocks of psalms attributed to David, which dominate the Psalter.

Clearly the connection made between David and the Psalms is a dominant feature of the book. It is certainly the literary feature that has had the most decisive effect on traditional Psalms interpretation. In every era, in ways consonant with the times, the connection with David has been a central hermeneutical principle. It is also the most difficult literary aspect of the book to assess. The connection between David and the Psalms is complex, composed of a variety of different elements. It has also diminished and been largely ignored since historical criticism severed the relation between the historical David and the composition of the psalms. But when the book is recognized as a guide to reading the psalms, the Davidic connection demands attention.

The person who reads the Psalter as part of the Old Testament knows of course who David is from the books of Samuel and Chronicles. David is the shepherd who was chosen to be the LORD's anointed king. The Psalter assumes that acquaintance. It opens up and develops dimensions of David that serve the purposes set out in the introduction.[5]

1. David is presented as one of the lowly, indeed as a person who is a model of the piety of those who depend on the LORD in the midst of the exigencies of life. The location of Psalm Three is crucial—as the first attributed to David, it sets the tone for all the rest.

It is a prayer of need and trust. In it speaks a person who depends on the LORD in the midst of overwhelming danger. The prayer proclaims that "salvation belongs to the LORD" (v. 8). It exemplifies the beatitude that concludes Psalm 2, "Happy are all who take refuge in him." The rest of the David psalms are predominantly expressions of reliance on the LORD, whether prayers or songs of thanksgiving or testimonies of trust. Sometimes it is difficult to determine their generic identity, but never their major theme. The David of the psalms enacts and illustrates and teaches a life lived by the steadfast love of the LORD. In the David psalms this king of Israel is identified as, and identifies with, the 'aniyyim, the lowly who say to the LORD, "I am poor and needy." The connection with David does not so much claim the psalms as the voice of a king as it identifies him, in the psalms that are claimed for David, with the lowly.

The heading of Psalm 3 connects it with the time "when he fled from his son Absalom." This reference is the first of thirteen narrative settings that appear in superscriptions. They also emphasize David's character as a vulnerable human, dependent on the LORD. The settings connect the psalms they introduce with incidents told in the books of Samuel. Eight of them refer to the period when David was threatened by Saul's hostility, before he was king. Of the four that refer to occasions after he became king, three deal also with times of failure and need. The superscription to Psalm 18, which also appears in 2 Samuel 22, contains a phrase that can serve as a summary for all the narrative settings: "When the LORD delivered him from the hand of all his enemies, and from the hand of Saul." The editorial purpose of the narrative settings is to make David the literary vehicle of a piety of dependence on the salvation of the LORD.

2. David is presented as the anointed of the LORD. He is the king whose kingship reflects and represents the reign of the LORD in the world and whose kingship is secured forever by the covenant promise of God. There are a number of psalms that speak of David in this way.[6] The way in which these psalms are set in the context of the book contributes significantly to how they may be understood.

The introductory Psalm 2 is the first of the psalms whose subject is the Davidic kingship and its relation to the reign of the LORD. It is a clear signal to pay attention to the others as a crucial topic of the book. David's kingship is an important manifestation and medium of the steadfast love of the LORD. The reader is invited not only to trust the LORD with David and like David, but also to trust the LORD because of David and through David. Here is torah that is proclamation to be believed rather than model to be followed. David as presented in these psalms is distinct from the reader. God works in and through David to claim the world for his kingship. The reign of the LORD is at stake in the destiny of David.

These psalms of David's kingship are not identified or grouped in the Psalter in any distinguishing way. They are instead scattered in an apparently random way throughout the book, so as to mingle them with the rest. Their random location ranges them along with all the other psalms of David. The effect is to keep this royal, messianic David in the context of the David who prays and praises as one of the lowly. The messiah is one of the lowly, and it is as a lowly one that he is king. The predominance of prayers of affliction as context in the book emphasizes this characterization; the Davidic king is a king who suffers opposition, persecution, accusation, betrayal, and pain. Indeed, some of the prayers give the clear impression that the suffering of the psalmic David is the occasion for a saving work of the LORD that will evoke and encourage the trust and hope of all the lowly. So David is not only portrayed as one of the lowly; he is also a sign of hope for the lowly.

There is one important exception in the location of psalms about the

Davidic kingship.[7] Psalm 89 concludes Book III. It is a long, fervent lament over the fall of the LORD's messiah and over the unfulfilled promise to David. It is followed at the beginning of Book IV by a grouping of psalms (90—100) that feature the theme and topic of the reign of the LORD, as if to say that the answer to the lament is secure in the everlasting and all-encompassing reign of God. Then, in Books IV and V, there are psalms that treat the kingship of David as a promise yet to be fulfilled (Psalms 110 and 132). A "once and future" perspective is thus set on the psalmic presentation of the kingship of David. An unmistakable relation to prophetic words about the Davidic king of the future emerges.

An important connection between the introductory Psalm 1 and the psalms on the Davidic kingship should be noted. The anointed king is portrayed as one who conforms to the instruction given at the book's beginning. The law of the LORD is the norm by which Davidic kings are to be judged (89:30–33). The king loves righteousness and hates wickedness (45:7). He keeps the ways of the LORD whose ordinances are always before him (18:20–22). When other psalms attributed to David are brought into consideration, like Psalms 15 and 19, the psalmic David appears as teacher and advocate of torah. In the Psalter as a whole, the messiah is one who keeps and teaches the torah and combines in his identity and role the two emphases of the twofold introduction to the Psalter.

3. David is presented as source and patron of praise and prayer for the worship of the LORD. This role is not itself the subject of psalms in the way the other identities are. It is, rather, implied and constructed out of elements of the superscriptions, the juxtaposition of David psalms with those of the Asaphites and Korahites, and the conclusion of the Psalter.

The superscriptions of the David psalms frequently contain items that identify the psalms as even more than the prayers and praise of David. They are classified by technical terms for public music, such as psalm, *shiggaion*, *miktam*, *maskil*, which mark them as pieces that have been used in general worship. There are instructions for performance, like "according to The Gittith" in the heading of Psalm 8. Many psalms are attributed "to the leader," a role probably connected with the performance of public worship (1 Chron. 15:21; also vv. 22, 27). These all indicate that the psalms collected in the book have a liturgical identity.

Besides the dominant blocks of David psalms, there are the groupings attributed to Asaph and the Korahites. These two are names known elsewhere, in Chronicles, as patronymics and guilds of Temple musicians appointed by David (See 1 Chron. 15—16). In the arrangement of the book, the second block of David psalms is set within concentric bands of Korahite and Asaph psalms to compose Books II and III of the Psalter. This association of David with Asaph and Korahites in the arrangement of the Psalter assumes and reflects the account of David's inauguration of worship, and especially of musical liturgy, in Jerusalem. The psalms may be read not only in the light of the David of Samuel, but also in the light of the David of Chronicles and of the authority and importance given to the community's worship of the LORD by David's authorization.

The way the book ends also contributes to this perspective on David and the psalms. The last David psalm is 145. It concludes with the resolution that "my mouth will speak the praise of the LORD, and all flesh will bless his holy name forever and ever" (145:21). The following five psalms all begin and end with "Praise the LORD," but have no superscription. As the sequel to Psalm 145, they represent in the book the fulfillment of David's resolve. The last psalm in the book ends with the summons, "Let everything that breathes praise the LORD." This final word of the book is an invocation. In it David calls on every human being to join in the praise of the LORD through the praise that he and Asaph and the Korahites offer. The Psalter is a torah of praise. To meditate on the psalms and recite them is to learn the praise of God in the profound sense of "learn." Through the Psalter, David leads the world in the praise of the LORD.

— V —

Any survey of the published works of those attempting to discern the literary character of the book of Psalms and what it means for reading the psalms soon leads to the realization that it is possible to take literary features in quite different ways. This approach is as fraught with problems as others are. It is well to be aware of the difficulties. Among the more important are these.

1. There does not seem to be one uniform literary shape or plan to the book into which everything fits, a literary scheme that accounts for everything. In following any particular pattern through the book, one comes on anomalies. An obvious illustration is the concluding note to Psalm 72, which says, "the prayers of David son of Jesse are ended," although there are quite a few prayers of David yet to come in the book. It is apparent that in the composition of the Psalter patterns of earlier groupings were overlaid by subsequent expansions. Various plans and arrangements have been combined and melded together in the larger whole, with their own individuality intact. The final shape seems to be a montage of patterns. Like the relation of David to the psalms, the book is complex, a literary world of different levels.

2. In a literary reading of the Psalter one is always in danger of overbidding the material, of imagining connections and patterns. Topics are so typical and language so formulaic in the world of the psalms that it is difficult to decide whether collocations and correspondences and contrasts are accidental or intentional, and if the latter, what to make of them.

3. Approaching the Psalter in a purely literary way, with the customary

historical questions bracketed out, is quite difficult, given the habits and interest of critical study. Indeed, one of the most interesting and important implications of literary features is what they suggest about the formation of the book. But as soon as one turns to a historical explanation for some feature of the book, or sets some part of it in an earlier period as interpretive context, the venture of interpretation has moved behind the book and its context. The use of contemporary form-critical categories for descriptive purposes also introduces considerations that do not appear to have played much of any role in arranging the psalms. But the habit of designating psalms by genre is so strong that descriptive analysis easily falls into the language of modern form criticism. The "royal psalm" as defined and understood in contemporary study was not a concept of the makers of the Psalter; they seem, rather, to have been concerned with content and vocabulary, in this case what a psalm said about kingship and David. Studying the Psalter and its psalms as a reader guided by content and arrangement, and using the other books of the Old Testament as secondary context, requires a practiced concentration.

4. While a literary reading requires one to hold historical questions and perspectives in abeyance, it cannot be thought to invalidate or replace the approaches that are useful in understanding the origins of the psalms and the formation of the Psalter. The conclusions of the other approaches condition and qualify the implications of the literary approach. A literary reading will attempt to take the attribution of Psalm 3 to David in all seriousness. But it is probably impossible to "think" David in the way traditional biographical or christological exegesis did. It is illegitimate for a literary reading of Psalm 3 to transform itself into a personal history or intentional typology; that outruns its warrants. What the approach does gain is an understanding of David, the chosen messiah, as one who prays as one of the lowly, and a relation to the psalm through David, who provides the psalm for the lowly to pray. This understanding of David and this purpose of the psalms belong to the realm of scripture, not biography and not prophecy. But both are surely more accessible to the use of the psalms in the New Testament and in the communities of faith than a construal of the psalm in cultic or historical contexts. It is a reading that reaches for an understanding that is there in the torah of the book.

# CHAPTER 13

# THE PLACE OF
# THE TORAH PSALMS
# IN THE PSALTER

Psalms 1, 19, and 119 are poems that differ in structure and content. But they are similar in one distinctive feature. They are psalms in which the instruction of the LORD is the central organizing topic.

This distinctive feature seems to make them oddities in the Psalter. In most introductory treatments of the book, Psalms 1, 19, and 119 are leftovers. They do not fit easily into any of the established genres or into any of the proposed orders for cultic procedures in ancient Israel. They are sometimes viewed as "wisdom psalms," but there is uncertainty about that classification.

Yet those who composed them wrote them *as psalms* and they were included *in the Psalter*. This double fact means that the latest and smallest group of the psalms may provide the central clue to the way the psalms, individually and as a book, were read and understood at the time of their composition and inclusion. The problem children of the Psalter do not have a place in the types and settings-in-life of psalm criticism, but they do have a place in the book.[1]

So the question of the torah psalms is not just a question of their interpretation as isolated pieces. It is also a question of what their presence in the book of Psalms means for the way the Psalms can be viewed and read. How do things look if the customary direction of analysis is reversed and one begins with these latest, leftover psalms and looks at them in the book and at the book through them? What effect does their presence have on other psalms and the way they are to be understood? What is their "place" in the Psalter?

We will look first at the psalms individually, then at their relationship to some other psalms, and finally at their location.

— I —

*The literary and theological character of the three psalms.* All are the work of poets who are bringing together elements of vocabulary, style, and theology

128

from various parts of the emerging Hebrew canon of scripture. This intentional mixing is a way of expressing a more comprehensive understanding of God and is the basic characteristic of such poetry. In each of these psalms there is a clue to how its author viewed the Psalter.

Psalm 1 connects the interpretation of Israel's past found in Deuteronomy–Kings with the question of how each person should live in the present to have a fortunate future.

In form, vocabulary, and topic Psalm 1 is a creation of the literary conventions found in Proverbs. But in its central subject matter the psalm is related to texts in the books of Joshua and Deuteronomy. The psalm describes the happy righteous as one whose concern is with the instruction of the LORD, and who therefore studies it constantly. The description is a variation of the LORD's instruction to Joshua when he succeeds Moses as leader of Israel, and of the law for kings in Deuteronomy 17.

The First Psalm, by echoing these texts, applies the instruction and lesson of that record to wisdom's question about how life is to be lived. The torah of the LORD replaces wisdom and its human teachers. The responsibility that once was primarily that of Israel's leaders is laid squarely on the shoulders of the pious.[2] In its introductory role, Psalm 1 is a signal of the importance of the Psalter for that piety and of torah-piety for the book of Psalms. All the categories by which the psalmists identify themselves and their circle—as servants, humble, fearers of the LORD, devoted ones—are to be understood in light of the First Psalm.

Psalm 19 brings together cosmos, torah, and prayer. It puts in an interrelated sequence the language of the heavens, the instruction of the LORD, and the words of the psalmist.

The psalm is a literary unit. The custom of dividing it into two or three separate units overlooks the compositional techniques uncovered in several recent studies, which unite quite different styles and topics.[3] To a strictly form-critical approach, the combinations seem artificial. But that is an indication that this poem and many others assigned to "mixed genres" are a type of literature whose generic characteristic is the gathering and combination of styles and materials into a new kind of unit.[4] The juxtaposition of cosmic speech with categories of the LORD's instruction is certainly intentional. The heavenly order praises God, and the psalmist praises the instruction of the LORD. The torah of the LORD is just as certain and everlasting, just as much a part of the nature of reality, as the succession of day and night and the regular course of the sun.

The literary model for the second part of Psalm 19 comes from Proverbs. The psalm commends the torah of the LORD in the same way that the teacher commends wisdom (Prov. 8:1–21; see also 4:20–23; 6:23), and claims for the torah of the LORD excellences and functions that include and surpass those of wisdom. To extend the commendation, the author has searched out and assembled five companion terms for torah: testimony, precepts, commandment, fear, and ordinance.[5] One can put it that way because the terms are at home in various kinds of literary sources, and the list and its order are unique. This eclectic gathering of terms is a procedure used also in Psalm 119.[6] It suggests that the psalmist found the instruction of the LORD in a variety of sources.

The concluding prayer knows about the dangers of "the unintended errors" dealt with in Leviticus 4—5 and of the insolent men who afflict the righteous in Psalm 119. The author asks to be kept innocent and free of these dangers, and offers his words and the meditation they express as the acceptable sacrifice to accompany his prayer. That is, the recited psalm performs a cultic function without the cultic procedures of sacrifice.[7] This is a clue to the way other psalms, the hymns and the prayers, are viewed by the composer. They are all words of mouth expressing meditation of heart said as the primary medium of worship.

Psalm 119 pushes the procedure of using torah as a center for organizing a variety of material to the limits possible for one literary unit. A large repertoire of genres and scripture material is combined into an expression of a piety that is the real setting of the psalm.[8] The formal framework of the whole is an acrostic arrangement with eight poetic lines to the letter. The topic of each of the lines is one of the terms that make up a vocabulary of torah. Line by line, all the various situations and moods that belong to the relation between the LORD and the servant of the LORD are dealt with, always with one of the torah terms as medium of the relationship. The result is a liturgical tapestry of devotional moves. The compositional technique has rightly been called anthological, but with the reservation that what has been created is no mere collection, but a combination that becomes a unity. Psalm 119 is the consummate mixed genre and a clue to what is going on in other psalms that do not fit the standard psalmic types.

The list of terms for torah is somewhat different from and longer than the list in Psalm 19. The practice of forming word clusters of this kind seems to begin in Deuteronomy–Kings, where the cluster is used to combine various kinds of legal sentences under the one rubric of torah.[9] But in Psalm 119 the list reflects not just the consolidation of various kinds of materials, as in Deuteronomy, but the assembling of various writings that provide access to the teaching of the LORD. The cluster of terms is not so much a list of synonyms that refer to one entity, but more a vocabulary that refers to a variety of writings that are regarded as having one function. The list is meant to include whatever serves as instruction about the way of the LORD and of his servants.

Moreover, the psalm is strewn with phrases that appear in other books of the Hebrew canon and in other psalms.[10] The poet repeatedly refers to searching, studying, reciting the material identified by his cluster of terms, a clue that he is quite aware of his sources and what he is doing.[11]

Within the acrostic structure the poetic lines form a generic montage of elements drawn from the principal types of psalms. The elements of the hymn, the thanksgiving, the lament, the song of confidence, the didactic poem are used in a way that seems somewhat controlled by the demands of the acrostic pattern and somewhat by immediate context. Within those constraints, the psalm praises the LORD, makes petitions, describes trouble, confesses need, makes vows, tells of salvation, asserts trust, describes the wicked, and so on. All this generic diversity is held together as though the one who addresses God through the psalm were himself in his trust and experience the life setting of it all. This combination of psalmic genres into speech with which the servant of the LORD speaks to God is a clue to the way the rest of the psalms are viewed. They are all particular cases of the way a servant addressed his divine LORD, themselves fragments of a larger whole brought together in Psalm 119.

— II —

*The relation of the torah psalms to other psalms.* These three, Psalms 1, 19, and 119, are the only psalms composed on the theme of torah, but they do not stand isolated in the Psalter. If one reads through the psalms prompted by the introductory claim that the instruction of the LORD is the concern of the righteous and the effective factor in determining how life comes out, other expressions of this theology can be found scattered throughout the Psalter. Fourteen psalms are involved;[12] taken with the primary three, that makes seventeen. They all belong to the last stratum of the collection, or have been developed by torah interests.

Taken together, this harvest of texts contains a profile of an understanding of the LORD's way with people and world that is organized around torah. Torah applies to everything.

It applies to the basic narrative that runs from the fathers to the land. The story of the LORD' way with his people is said to have its meaning and purpose in his instruction.

Torah applies to the offices of priest and king. Moses, Aaron, and Samuel, the original sequence of priests, responded to the speech of God by observing the testimonies and statutes he gave them (Ps. 99:6–7). The LORD's covenant with David will endure, but always David's sons will be under the discipline of the LORD's torah in ordinances, statutes, and commandments (89:30–33).

Torah applies to Israel's future. It is a condition of the continuity of the LORD's steadfast love and faithfulness to Israel. Torah applies to the life of every person. The lesson learned from the teachers of wisdom that it is well for the righteous and bad for the wicked is understood in the light of torah as the source of wisdom.

Torah applies even to the LORD's creating and ordering the elements of the world. The commanding word that brought forth the earth to endure (33:6–9) and sends winter and summer (147:15–19) is described by the same vocabulary and put in direct sequence with the LORD's word in statutes and ordinances to Israel.

It is not difficult to imagine how this unifying point of view, stated as an introduction to the Psalter and reiterated across its breadth, could provide a perspective from which the rest of the Psalter could be understood and read. In fact, Psalm 119 is a poetic inventory of the ways in which the instruction of the LORD in all its categories can become the agenda for virtually all the functions of psalmic hymn and prayer. In this way of thinking, just as torah has taken over the functions of wisdom, the life concerned with torah is lived in psalmic functions. The coherence of the Psalter with its introduction becomes clearer. The psalms are the liturgy for those whose concern and delight is the torah of the LORD.

It also becomes clearer why study of the torah is said in the introduction to be the characteristic of the righteous. How does one come to be able to praise and pray and act out of the center of torah? Three times in the Psalter we hear of the person on whose mind and emotions torah is, as it were, imprinted.[13] The instructing word has been incorporated in the very structure of consciousness by a kind of study mentioned in all three of the torah psalms.[14] It is a kind of study that proceeds orally; it rehearses and repeats. It searches the instruction of God by reciting in receptivity until the matter becomes part of the thinking and willing and doing. For this kind of discipline, any text that has become scripture can become instruction, command, word, precept.

— III —

*The location of the torah psalms in the Psalter.* Psalm 1 is only half of the introduction to the book. It is generally recognized that Psalms 1 and 2 together form a literary unit.[15] The combination brings together the topics of torah and the kingship of the LORD. One part addresses the question of the individual; the other, of history. One is concerned with the problem of the wicked in society, the other with the nations of the world. There is a choice between two ways for the individual (one can scoff at torah or delight in it) and for the nations (one can rebel or one can serve the LORD). This intricate pairing as introduction says that all the psalms dealing with the living of life under the LORD must be understood and recited in the light of the reign of the LORD, and all psalms concerned with the kingship of the LORD are to be understood and recited with the torah in mind.

It is also generally agreed that by the time the Psalter was being completed, the psalms dealing with the kingship of the LORD were understood eschatologically.[16] They no longer refer only to what was enacted in cult, but refer as well to what was promised in prophecy. Psalm 2, reread as a vision of the goal of history, puts the torah-piety of Psalm 1 in an eschatological context. The end of the wicked and the vindication of the righteous can be understood in terms of the coming kingdom of God. The compositional pairing of the two psalms is a work of theological synthesis, a combining of literary entities that reflects an intellectual consolidation of the resources of Pentateuch, prophecy, and wisdom in psalmic form.

There are other cases in the Psalter of composing and arranging psalms in pairs to bring topics together to create a more comprehensive theological statement.[17] Psalms 111 and 112 are a set of two, both in the acrostic form, and clearly composed to complement each other. Psalm 111 summarizes the deeds of the LORD and concludes with the point that "the beginning of wisdom is the fear of the LORD." Psalm 112 commends the one who fears the LORD by delighting in his commandments, and concludes with a contrast with the wicked. The ways of God and the ways of the righteous are paired.

Psalms 105 and 106 are both narrative hymns. The first surveys the wondrous works of the LORD and makes the point that the LORD's purpose was that Israel should keep his laws (v. 45). The second surveys the same history as a recitation of Israel's faithlessness throughout, and makes the point that Israel's salvation depends on the LORD's great faithfulness. The righteousness of God and the sinfulness of Israel are paired.

Psalms 9 and 10 are a continuous, though broken, acrostic of two parts. The first, using the style of thanksgiving, deals with God's way with the wicked nations. The second, using the style of lament, deals with God's way with wicked people. In the midst of each, the kingship of God is announced (9:8 and 10:12), and from each the cry "Arise, O LORD" (9:20 and 10:16) is heard. All the psalms appearing as pairs have thematic connections with the three torah psalms.

This raises the question of whether Psalms 19 and 119 are also located so each stands in correlation with another psalm. Is it a mere accident that both, with their emphasis on torah as the center of life, follow a psalm in which, as in Psalm 2, the problem is the nations against whom the LORD acts to save the righteous one as a vindication of his sovereignty? Is it fortuitous that both Psalms 18 and 118 are subject to an eschatological rereading? There are features of content and motif that suggest an intentional pairing. In the case of 18 and 19, both begin with a cosmic theophany that reveals the power of God (18:8–16 and 19:2–7). Psalm 18 says the way of God is perfect and the word of the LORD is pure (v. 31), and Psalm 19 says the instruction of the LORD is perfect and the commandment of the LORD is pure (vv. 8, 9). Psalm 118 tells of the salvation of a rejected righteous one, which vindicates the faith of the righteous. Psalm 119 is a prayer for salvation by the righteous who are rejected on account of faithfulness to torah. These are only illustrations of the connecting features to be found.

In all three cases, the purpose of the pairing seems to be the provision of an eschatological context for a piety based in torah. Those who are at work in the final shaping and arrangement of the Psalter are completely committed to torah as the divinely willed way of life. Their theology said that "the LORD knows the way of the righteous, but the way of the wicked will perish" (Ps. 1:6). But things did not work out that way in their experience. The Psalter is itself full of evidence that it doesn't. Those who trust in the LORD suffer. The righteous are afflicted. Prayers for help go up as the liturgy of the pious. Yet nowhere in the final content of the Psalter is this faith surrendered. It is tried and questioned, but neither the way of Job nor the way of Ecclesiastes is followed. The reason is the eschatological context of the torah-piety—the hope for the coming kingdom of God.

## — IV —

The three points considered above sketch an approach to the Psalms which begins with the torah psalms. These considerations show that much appears in a different light when these psalms are allowed to provide an introduction to and perspective on the rest. To take up the torah psalms as the problem children of the Psalter is in the end to take up the question of the entire book of Psalms. Implications, possibilities, and questions are uncovered that do not usually arise in other approaches.

The context for the construal of language in the psalms shifts. Semantic horizons are more those of intratextual relations and less groups of types and reconstructed cultic occasions. Form-critical and cult-functional questions are subordinated, and questions of content and theology become more important. The so-called mixed type of psalm takes on an important role as clue to the way the psalms are to be viewed and understood.

The torah psalms point to a type of piety as setting in life for the psalms, a piety that used the entire book as prayer and praise. That means this piety was quite different from any self-righteous, single-minded legalism. Its basic religious commitments were devotion to the instruction of the LORD and trust in the reign of the LORD. The two primary problems with which it lived were wickedness in self and society and the arrogance and power of the nations. The questions with which it wrestled were the incongruity of conduct and experience and the hiddenness of the purpose of God in history. Its way was faithfulness through study and obedience and hope through prayer and waiting. The psalms were reread in the light of this piety, and the piety in turn was constantly shaped by the use of the psalms.

If there is a bit of cogency to this approach to the Psalter, it is an illustration in the field of criticism of the eschatological proverb, "The last will be first, and the first last."

# CHAPTER 14

# PSALM 118 IN THE LIGHT OF CANONICAL ANALYSIS

In his *Introduction to the Old Testament as Scripture,* Brevard Childs proposes a fundamental shift in the practice of criticism.[1] Under the rubric of canon, he has laid out an approach to the books of the Old Testament that relativizes the methodological questions and values of historical criticism. The consequences of this approach for the interpretation of particular texts are of the greatest importance for exegesis. In works that preceded and led to his *Introduction,* Childs provided examples of exegetical work,[2] but it is the *Introduction* that brings his work to summation and lays out a full statement of its theoretical bases.

This chapter is an attempt to interpret a text in light of the *Introduction.* It is certainly not meant to be an illustration of "how to practice Childs's method." The *Introduction* does not propose, strictly speaking, an exegetical method or model. Childs is quite clear that "a canonical introduction is not the end, but only the beginning of exegesis. . . . The canon establishes a platform from which exegesis is launched. . . . A variety of different exegetical models" can be based on canonical analysis. But it is canonical analysis of the books of the Old Testament that supplies the assumptions and directions with which exegesis should work.[3]

— I —

*Choice of the text.* Psalm 118 has been chosen as the text for our exegesis because it has established liturgical settings in Judaism and Christianity. Jews and Christians have from ancient times recited and heard Psalm 118 in the hermeneutical context of special occasions. These liturgical settings show how the psalm has been used and understood. Judaism knows the psalm as the last in the "Hallel," Psalms 113—118, which had been used in the celebration of the joyous festivals since before the turn of the eras. Psalm 118 in particular had a prominent role in the festival of Tabernacles (Mishnah

*Sukkah* 4:1, 8) and in the ceremonies of Passover, both at the Temple (Mishnah *Pesaḥim* 5:7) and at the household meal (ibid., 8:3; 10:6). In Christianity, Psalm 118 was used from earliest times in worship on Sunday, "the day the LORD has made" (Ps. 118:24) by the resurrection of Jesus Christ. When the annual celebration of Easter Sunday developed, the psalm was said in the order of the principal service, a practice that continues to the present time in the liturgy of most Christian churches.

In both traditions the psalm is understood as a text that speaks of the salvation on which the existence of the community is based. For the Jews it is the exodus and all that symbol represents in their scripture and tradition; for Christians it is the crucifixion and resurrection of Jesus Christ. One of Childs's concerns, a point made repeatedly in his *Introduction*, is that modern historical criticism has tended to distance biblical texts from their use in theology and liturgy. The traditional liturgical use of Psalm 118 provides a pole of comparison against which to view an exegesis undertaken on the basis of canonical analysis. Is the resulting interpretation more open to and helpful to the use of the psalm in a community of faith and practice?

*Description of the text.* It is useful to begin with a description of the psalm drawn in as methodologically neutral a way as possible. Every approach, as a project in understanding and explaining, begins with a unit of language that has a presumed logical structure. The logical structure consists of the arrangement of the clauses of a text by means of verbal meaning, syntax, and discourse style, the elements accessible to any careful reading of the text.

Psalm 118 opens and concludes with plural imperatives invoking grateful praise of the LORD for the goodness of his everlasting *ḥesed* (vv. 1, 29). It is introduced by three jussive sentences (vv. 2–4) calling Israel, the house of Aaron, and those who fear the LORD to "say" that the LORD's *ḥesed* is enduring, apparently as the aggregate group addressed by verse 1. The rest of the psalm can be read in two parts, verses 5–18 and 19–28.

The first part is concerned with the salvation that has happened. The style is first-person singular, referring to the LORD in the third person. Twice the speaker reports that the LORD delivered him from distress (vv. 5 and 13). Each report is followed by statements about the LORD and about the situation created for the speaker by the LORD's help (vv. 6–12 and 14–18). Whether verses 10–12 are thus appropriately described depends on the full explanation of the text.

The second part of the text is concerned with an entry made by one who has been saved (vv. 19–20, 26, and probably 27). The first-person style continues in verses 18–20 and 28, and becomes direct address to the LORD in verses 21 and 28. In verses 23–27, the first singular changes to plural. The psalm continues to make statements about and to the LORD, and about the situation in the light of the LORD's deliverance (vv. 21–24, 27a, 28). There is also a prayer (v. 25), a blessing (v. 26), and an instruction (v. 27b).

*Psalm 118 in modern criticism.* Modern criticism has been primarily interested in psalms as individual texts, and has viewed the book as the result of a
process of collecting and expanding that has little significance for the
interpretation of particular psalms. They are understood instead in terms of a
genre and of cultic proceedings. For those who emphasize form criticism,
genre analysis is likely to be decisive; proposals about *Sitz im Leben* tend to
flow from classification; decisions about ambiguous verbal meanings follow.
For those who emphasize the character of the psalms as cultic songs, a
hypothesis about the cultic life of Judah in the preexilic period is decisive;
proposals about the use of a particular psalm depend on its relation to the
hypothesis, and the construal of obscure verbal meanings follows.

The two parts of Psalm 118 provide a purchase for each of the emphases.
Verses 5–18, with their report and celebration of a deliverance from distress,
are generally classified as the thanksgiving of an individual. Verses 19–28,
with their mixture of entrance rituals, prayer, blessings, and shift between
singular and plural, are generally recognized as a liturgy for the completion of
rites in which the individual gives praise for deliverance (verses 19, 21, 28).
For Hermann Gunkel, genre was decisive.[4] The psalm is a thanksgiving for a
private individual who has brought his celebration into the midst of the
congregation. The trouble that threatened death was sickness. The apparent
military language in verses 10–12 and 15–16 is used metaphorically. For
Sigmund Mowinckel, the psalm is an entrance liturgy used in the fall festival
for the enthronement of Yahweh.[5] The individual voice is that of a representative king or leader. The trouble from which the singer has been rescued
from life to death is the typical compound of enemies, natural disasters, etc.,
which the nation has come through. The interpretations of Gunkel and
Mowinckel are illustrative of lines generally taken in contemporary criticism
with various modulations.[6] But overall, genre and cultic use in shifting
relationships are decisive for the construal of verbal meanings. The psalm is
understood and interpreted as an artifact of ritual proceedings in Judah.

*The psalm as scripture.* For the approach developed in Childs's *Introduction*,
"scripture" is the controlling rubric. It subordinates both genre and cultic
setting as directive concepts for exegesis. Scripture is *what* a text is, and *where*
it is. "Canonical analysis" leads to exegetical practice that recognizes that fact
and follows its implications. The interests and concerns of such practice for an
exegesis of Psalm 118 would include the following.[7]

1. The text is part of the book of Psalms, which was shaped in its present
arrangement and content to serve as scripture. The book is the first interpretive horizon for the psalm, rather than the genres of speech used in ancient
Israel or the history of its cult. Exegesis will seek to read the language of the
psalm under the constraints and directives of the book.

2. The book of Psalms stands within a larger collection of scripture, which
forms a second interpretive horizon. The language of Psalm 118 will be

understood in terms of possibilities offered by the canon of scriptures, rather than those provided by proposed periods, reconstructed rituals, or precanonical views of God and his ways. For instance, such matters as the central importance of torah or prophetic eschatology may come into play in making sense of the language of the psalm, even though such elements may not have been operative in the hypothetical precanonical context in which the psalm was written and used.

3. Psalm 118 in the Masoretic text of the book of Psalms is the text for interpretation.[8] The Masoretic text will be preferred over reconstructions based on earlier systems of language. The present form of the text will control the interpretation, rather than reference to any possible earlier reconstructed forms.

4. The concept of scripture incorporates a reference to a community whose recognition of its authority and use as instruction about the way of God and the way to live belong to its identity. That community is the historical setting of Psalm 118 that exegesis has to consider.[9] Exegesis will attempt to understand the psalm as a reader would have in the historical group for whom the *Tehillim* became scripture. Because of the character of Psalm 118, and the other psalms, it must be added that the focus on scripture as identity does not exclude consideration of the liturgical use of the psalm as scripture. The approach is open to considering the use of the psalm in worship, where its understanding is under the constraints and direction of its identity as scripture.

— II —

*The beginning and end of the psalm.* As part of its own shape, the psalm begins (v. 1) and ends (v. 29) with a summons to offer grateful praise to the LORD because of the goodness shown in his everlasting *ḥesed.* The inclusion of the psalm within the parentheses of this summons interprets the whole as a testimony and response to a manifestation of the LORD's *ḥesed.* That is what is happening through all the telling in the psalm about deliverance and its meaning. The summons appears in three other psalms and in three other books of the canon (Pss. 106:1; 107:1; 136:1; 1 Chron. 16:34; 2 Chron. 20:21; Jer. 33:11). The psalms tell how the LORD's *ḥesed* delivered Israel from faithlessness (Ps. 106), situations of distress (Ps. 107), and the chaos of cosmos and history (Ps. 136). The narrative settings locate the hymn in the celebration of the Ark's entry into Jerusalem (1 Chron. 16:34) and in a battle against the nation's foes (2 Chron. 20:21). Jeremiah 33:11 says it is the song of thanks that the gathered nation will sing in the time when the LORD restores the fortunes of the land. In every case the hymn appears in texts that speak of actions of the LORD that concern the community, rather than an individual. All three of the psalms end in language that connects the past saving acts of the LORD with the situation of the congregation after the return from exile (Pss. 106:44–47; 107:33–41; 136:23–24). The congregation is composed of delivered people who pray for the completion of salvation (106:47), as does Psalm 118 (see v. 25).

*The participants.* Verses 2–4 give a threefold identification of those who are to speak of the *ḥesed* of the LORD: Israel, house of Aaron, fearers of the LORD. The same inclusive list appears twice in a nearby psalm (115:9–13; also in 135:19) to identify first-person plural pronouns. Psalm 118 has no title attributing the psalm to anyone; reader and singer of the psalm as scripture will take this group as antecedent of the first-person pronouns in verses 5–19, 21, 28; note the combination of singular and plural for the recipients of blessing in verse 26. The designation "those who fear the LORD" will not be read simply as a term for cultic participants. The term will assume the meaning of torah-piety rehearsed endlessly in Psalm 119 (see v. 38), where response to and hope in Yahweh's *ḥesed* turns around a relation to his torah. The understanding of *ṣaddiqim* in verses 15, 20 is also affected. The translation "victorious" used in some versions and commentaries assumes a military setting for the psalm. The setting of the book supports "righteous" and draws on the understanding of the righteous present in such psalms as 1, 19, 111, 112, and 119, among others.

*The salvation.* The two reports of past distress and the LORD's help are composed in metaphors and general language. Verse 5 speaks of the distress of being hemmed in, which the LORD relieved by a widening out. Verse 13 tells of having been pressed to the point of falling when helped by the LORD. The language could, as is typical of the plasticity of psalmic poetry, be used of a variety of predicaments and experiences. For guidance about the references of these reports, the denotative and connotative import of the words, one can turn to the rest of the psalm read as a unit and to its connections with other scripture.

1. The psalm speaks about salvation in language that appears also in the song sung by Moses and the Israelites (Ex. 15:1–18) after "the LORD *saved* Israel *that day* from the hand of the Egyptians; and Israel *saw* the Egyptians dead upon the seashore. And Israel *saw* the great work . . . , and the people *feared* the LORD; and they believed in the LORD and in his servant Moses" (Ex. 14:30–31, emphases added), all this after the people had complained that they were about "to *die* in the wilderness" (Ex. 14:11, emphasis added). The words here italicized in this introduction to Israel's song appear also in Psalm 118: *save* in verses 14, 21, 25; *day* as the time of the LORD's action in verse 24; *saw* as the verb for looking on foes in confidence in verse 7; *feared the LORD* as the identification of the singers in verse 4; *die* as the fate of Israel in verse 17. Israel's song is spoken in the first-person singular.

Moreover, Psalm 118 uses crucial sentences from Exodus 15. "The LORD is my strength and song, and he has become my salvation" (Ex. 15:2a, RSV) appears in verse 14 and in part in verse 21. A version of Exodus 15:2b occurs in verse 28. Both songs praise "the right hand of the LORD" and his prowess (Ex. 15:6, 12, and Ps. 118:15–16). Both speak of nations that can be faced in confidence because of the LORD's might displayed in salvation (Ex. 15:14–16 and Ps. 118:10–12). All these repetitions and relationships can be taken as directives that Psalm 118 is to be read and understood in light of the situation of Israel and of Israel's song in Exodus 14—15. Song and situation are not identical with the psalm, but when the ambiguous language of the psalm is read in the light of the Exodus situation and song, much is decided.

2. The grateful declaration of the psalm that "I shall not die, but live; and I shall tell the works of Yah" (v. 17) is to be understood in light of the prophetic proclamation that Israel would die (e.g., Amos 2:2; Hos. 13:1; Ezek. 18:31). As the claim of an individual, the declaration could be only temporary, for the time being. But as the faith of the community restored from dispersion and exile, it could be unconditional. They know now that the people of the LORD will not cease to exist. The account of deliverance from death to life in Psalm 116:8–9 is to be understood in the same way, and it is in relation to this understanding of death that statements that "the dead do not praise the LORD" (115:17–18; 30:8–10; 6:4–5) are to be understood. It is a matter of concern in the psalms because the death of the people of God would bring the praise of the LORD from human voices to a total halt, and that would be a contradiction of the LORD's entire way with Israel and the world. No praise would mean no recognition of the kingship or the character of the LORD.

*The situation.* In Psalm 118 the community that has been brought from death to life continues in predicament. Though they were saved, they pray for salvation (v. 25). Yet their situation has changed. Before the LORD's deliverance they faced death; now they face life. What they have learned from salvation is a faith with which they confront the threats of life. The psalm describes that faith in verses 6–12 in a way that suggests that the psalm is as much a song of confidence for the present as praise for what has happened in the past. The statement unfolds in three parts (vv. 6–7, 8–9, 10–12), which are mutually interpretive and can also be read under the guidance of other Old Testament texts.

1. The basic confession of faith is: "The LORD is for me; I am not afraid." Deliverance has brought knowledge ("This I know, that God is for me," Ps. 56:10). And it has brought confidence: those who have been saved are liberated from terror. This basic faith allows the community to view its situation in terms of a radical alternative laid out by putting the LORD in a contrasting pair first with "man/those who hate me" (118:6–7) and then with "man/leaders" (vv. 7–8). This theological strategem of describing a situation by a contrast between the LORD and *'adam* is used in several other texts. In Isaiah 31:3, the Egyptians are called "man/flesh" in contrast to "God," in a saying against those who trust Egypt instead of the LORD. Isaiah 51:7–8,

11–12 uses the contrast as a basis for a comforting call not to fear the human dangers that threaten Israel. Asa, facing war with the Ethiopians, prayed, "O LORD, you are our God; don't let man prevail against you." See also Jeremiah 17:5–8, and Psalms 9—10, 56, 124, and 146. The stratagem is a way to raise the question of Israel's faith in history to the level of an issue between the LORD and "man." The deliverance of the community has disclosed the LORD's commitment, and now history is viewed from that vantage.

2. A review of all these texts suggests that Ps. 118:10–12 should be read as a continuation of the statement of confidence, rather than as a report about a past victory over the nations. "*All* nations surround me"—that is the community's ongoing situation. "It is by the name of the LORD that I can ward them off"—that is the community's confidence. The situation is: God-fearing, LORD-trusting Israel in the midst of the nations. It is the nations who are spoken of under the terms "man . . . those who hate me . . . leaders," and it is in a life delivered from death but still lived among the nations that the community in this psalm praises and prays.

3. This clarification casts light on the saying in verse 22. "The stone which the builders rejected" is the community "hated" (in Hebrew, more an act than an emotion) by the nations. The LORD's salvation has revealed that the rejected are the focus and center of the LORD's way in the world. One notes how very near to Isaiah 53 these thoughts are.

4. Verse 18 draws another implication for the experience of distress, calling on the LORD, and deliverance. The distress brought on by human historical agents is taken to be the chastisement and discipline of the LORD. Psalm 66 uses the same interpretation of "my/our" suffering from the violence of "men." The reasoning runs that because the affliction did not lead to death, it was the work, not of God's final anger, but of his chastisement (see Pss. 6:2; 38:2; 119:67, 71). The book of Jeremiah applies this way of thinking to Judah's affliction by the Babylonians (Jer. 10:24; 30:11; 31:18). This theological reading of the community's past distress casts light on a textual problem in Ps. 118:13. The Masoretic text reads "*You* pressed me hard" (emphasis added), in a context in which there is no antecedent for this direct address. Some of the versions, followed by most translations, relieve the difficulty with a change to "*I* was hard pressed" (emphasis added). But though the Masoretic text's jag in style seems awkward, the thought makes perfect sense in this context: The LORD pressed his people to the point of falling in chastisement, but then helped them.

*The entry*. Verses 19–28 are concerned with an entry (vv. 19, 20, 26). Demonstrative sentences indicate the place and the time. The place is the gates of righteousness (v. 19), so called because the gates belong to the LORD and may be entered by the righteous (v. 20). The gates open into the house of the LORD, a place of blessing for those who enter (v. 20). The time for the entry is "the day which the LORD has made (v. 24). The purpose of the entry is to offer grateful praise directly to the LORD for his salvation (vv. 21, 28), the act that has created the day (vv. 22–24). This much is said by the text about the entry.

1. The psalm itself offers no help in connecting this entry with any particular cultic occasion or festival or historical event. The psalm has no title. There is no certain connection between its text and any probable setting. Its incorporation in the Psalter as scripture (as Childs repeatedly reminds us in the *Introduction*) has loosed it from any particular historical context and blurred its relation to any specific cultic proceeding. To reconstruct an occasion or a ritual as a context for understanding the entry would be to resort to a form-critical or cult-functional hypothesis. What one can say about it as a text in the *Tehillim* is simply that those who read it and used it in the community of the canon would have understood it as a text of praise for the remembered salvation of exodus and return by which the community, corporately and individually, expressed gratitude and iterated the faith by which they lived in the midst of the nations. Its connection with the Temple as the place where one came to be in the presence of the LORD would have been obvious in the context of the other psalms.

2. Because the community of Psalm 118 lives in the midst of the nations, it also expresses its trust in a prayer: *'anna' Yhwh hoši'ah na'* (v. 25). The saved community still prays for and yearns for salvation yet to occur. This prayer is a reason to consider some connections between Psalm 118 and the book of Isaiah. Chapter 11 of Isaiah concludes with a prophecy (vv. 11–16) that "the LORD will extend his hand yet a second time to recover the remnant that is left of his people," who are scattered in a dispersion among the nations (v. 11). Then, chapter 12 follows with a song of grateful praise in two parts (vv. 1–3 and 4–6), each introduced by the phrase "and you will say in that day." The songs to be sung in the day when the dispersion comes to Zion use language found in Exodus 15, in much the same way that Psalm 118 does. Exodus 15:2a appears in Isaiah 12:2b (see Ps. 118:14). Exodus 15:2b is reflected in Isaiah 12:5. In these hymns the scenario of a future salvation is similar to that found in Psalm 118: The LORD's anger has ended; he has become their salvation in event and song; they trust rather than fear; the setting is the nations of the earth.

In Isaiah 26 there is a song that will be sung "in that day" in the land of Judah. The song celebrates a strong city, with salvation as its walls (v. 1). Its *gates* are to open "that the *righteous* nation which practices faithfulness may *enter*" (v. 2, emphasis added). "That day" will arrive when the LORD has brought down the institution of human arrogance (v. 5) and vindicated "the way of the righteous" (v. 7).

These eschatological songs in Isaiah sketch a profile of the salvation prayed for in Psalm 118:25. They provide another interpretive horizon within the canon for the "entry" that takes place in verses 19–28. The entry of the righteous through the gates of the Temple anticipates the coming of the dispersed people to Zion. "The day that the LORD has made" is informed not only by the memory of salvation past but also by the hope of salvation to come. Psalmody and eschatological prophecy are brought together for the community by the interplay of scripture within the canon.

— III —

*Conclusions.* Reading the psalm under the direction and constraints of a canonical approach does result in an interpretation that has a rather distinctive profile.

1. The procedures followed and the conclusions reached in this exegesis overlap in certain details those found in almost all the studies of Psalm 118 surveyed by the writer. Probably a common text and the basic requirements of understanding language would guarantee that much. But the interpretation as a whole does, when compared, have distinctive contours. The questions that arise in the process of exegesis return to those found in the commentaries of a Luther or a Calvin (and even, at times, of the Midrash on Psalm 118) more often than do modern critical commentaries. The procedures and conclusions find their closest kin in the work of those for whom "relecture" (rereading) and "anthological" are themes of their approach.[10]

2. Psalm 118 is understood as a song for grateful praise to the LORD for his salvation. The praise is rendered by testimony to that salvation and to its effect on the saved, and by coming into the presence of the LORD to thank him. The salvation is the marvelous work of the LORD by which he delivered his people from death. The deliverance is described and interpreted in terms used elsewhere in the Hebrew canon for exodus and for the return from exile. The purpose of the text is not so much to celebrate a specific occurrence as it is to express the situation in which the LORD's saving activity, known from the larger scope of the canon, has put those who study and sing the psalm.

3. The historical context in which the psalm is read and used in this way is a religious community whose view of God, world, and self is created by the scriptures of the canon read in interrelationship. The thought-world of the community is reconstructed by undertaking to read the psalm as a unit prompted by the connections of its language and thought with other psalms in the final form of the Psalter and with other texts in the canon. The interpretation is meant to be descriptive and historical for that context. The usual procedure of criticism is to set portions of the Hebrew Bible in different periods arranged in chronological sequence, and to understand their individuality as a function of different times and social situations. Canonical analysis locates the text at the conclusion of the whole process, in a community for whom the whole is revelation. One cannot assume historically that there was only one way of reading scripture within the postexilic Jewish community at

any time. In that sense, "the community of the canon" is idealized, and it is reconstructed. But positing that community is the only way to think of a setting in life and in history for the genre "scripture" composed of the collection and final form of the books in the Hebrew canon.

4. The "I" is understood in terms of the "we." The theological identity is corporate. Note the use of first-person songs for the people in narrative and prophetic contexts in the Old Testament (e.g., Exodus 15, Isaiah 12). This does not cancel the function of the first-person style or eliminate the reading and use of the psalm by individuals. Psalm 56, which is similar in language and scenario, is attributed to a setting in David's life. What is happening in the interplay of scripture is a correlation of corporate and individual identities. David's narrative is taken as illustration and instruction about the people's life under God. Through David and the first-person style of the psalms, individuals understand their own existence in terms of the faith of the community. The issue is not a mutually exclusive choice between individual or corporate readings. The issue is whether individuals and community are understood by means of God's way, known through Exodus and exile and the people's response as laid out in the canon of scripture.

5. The ambiguous language in the psalm is construed in a way that is coherent with the psalm as a whole and meaningful in the context of the community of the canon. The talk about deliverance from death, the celebration in the tents of the righteous, the nations round about, and the prayer for salvation are not tied to a particular historical occasion or social setting or festival, but are read as functions of the canon. This opens the psalm to use and interpretation in later, different times by the community for whom the canon of scripture is the guide to faith and life. The testimonies to the salvation of the LORD in all of the canon are echoed in this language. It is a reading that seems to be coherent with its use in the joyous festivals of Judaism. Its use by the church puts the event of Jesus Christ in the sequence of the LORD's marvelous works of salvation and provides language for the Christian community to speak of the meaning of that salvation for their present and future.

# Notes

## 1. With These Words

1. For a recent comprehensive discussion of the translation of the sentence and its implications, see Marc Zvi Brettler, *God Is King*, Journal for the Study of the Old Testament Supplement Series, 76 (Sheffield: Sheffield Academic Press, 1989), 125–58.

2. T.N.D. Mettinger describes the symbol "King" as a root metaphor that provides an organizational matrix for a whole cosmos of ideas and lies behind the surface of many texts that do not even employ royal terms. He thinks the metaphor makes an important claim to be the center of the Old Testament understanding of God. See his *In Search of God* (Philadelphia: Fortress Press, 1988), 92–122.

3. See Sallie McFague's illuminating discussion of "the Kingdom of God made known in the parables and Jesus as a parable of God" in *Metaphorical Theology* (Philadelphia: Fortress Press, 1982). Chapter 4 is particularly pertinent.

4. In a review of Sallie McFague's *Metaphorical Theology*, P. D. Miller, Jr., exposes the flaw in the assumption that the kingship of God in the Old Testament is a projection of human kingship on God (*Journal of Biblical Literature* 3/1 [spring 1992]: 120–22).

5. See *Yhwh malak* in Pss. 93:1; 96:10; 97:1; 99:1; 146:10. *'Elohim malak* in 47:8.

6. See the fuller exposition of this thesis in chapter 2.

7. Thorkild Jacobsen, *The Treasures of Darkness* (New Haven, Conn.: Yale University Press, 1976).

## 2. The Center of the Psalms

1. See the recent introduction to the subject in Klaus Seybold, *Introducing the Psalms* (Edinburgh: T. & T. Clark, 1990).

2. For instance, Erhard Gerstenberger, "Still, the Psalter is so vast in its theological dimensions that any systematizing effort must fall short." *Psalms*, Part 1, The Forms of the Old Testament Literature, 14 (Grand Rapids: Wm. B. Eerdmans Publishing Co., 1988), 36.

3. Two important, quite different treatments are: H.-J. Kraus, *Theology of the Psalms*, trans. Keith Crim (Minneapolis: Augsburg Publishing House 1986); and H.

147

Spieckermann, *Heilsgegenwart. Eine Theologie der Psalmen* (Göttingen, 1989), who provides, in pp. 7–20, a survey of the recent approaches to the problem of describing the theology of the psalms.

4. On the question of a center around which to organize Old Testament theology, see the discussion and literature cited in H. D. Preuss, *Theologie des Alten Testaments*, vol. 1 (Stuttgart, Berlin, and Cologne, 1991), 25–30.

5. T.N.D. Mettinger calls the designation of Yhwh as King in the Old Testament "a root metaphor . . . a genetic code for a broad complex of ideas . . . a metaphor that generates other related metaphors." *In Search of God* (Philadelphia: Fortress Press, 1988), 92.

6. For a recent compilation of literature on the question, see chap. 6 and its notes in M. Z. Brettler, *God Is King*, Journal for the Study of the Old Testament Supplement Series, 76 (Sheffield: Sheffield Academic Press, 1989), 125–58.

7. A bibliography of the important works dealing with Yhwh as king is given in Preuss, *Theologie*, 123–74.

8. Psalms 5:2; 10:16; 24:7–10; 29:10; 44:4; 47:2, 6, 7; 48:2; 68:24; 74:12; 84:13; 95:3; 98:6; 99:4; 145:1; 149:2.

9. Psalms 9:4, 7; 22:28; 89:14; 103:19; 145:11–13.

10. On the union of these various roles, see Patrick D. Miller, Jr., "The Sovereignty of God," in *The Hermeneutical Quest*, ed. Donald G. Miller (Allison Park, Pa.: Pickwick Publications, 1986), 129–44; Brettler, *God Is King*, chaps. 3 and 4.

11. On the exegesis of this group of psalms, see especially J. Jeremias, *Das Königtum Gottes in den Psalmen*, Forschungen zur Religion und Literatur des Alten und Neuen Testaments, 141 (Göttingen: Vandenhoeck & Ruprecht, 1987), and M. E. Tate, *Psalms 51—100* (Word Biblical Commentary, 20; Dallas: Word, 1990). G. H. Wilson concludes that Psalms 90—106, which feature the kingship of Yhwh, "function as the editorial 'center' of the final form of the Hebrew Psalter." *The Editing of the Hebrew Psalter*, SBL Dissertation Series, 76 (Chico, Calif.: Scholars Press, 1985), 215.

12. On this scenario, its relation to mythic tradition in the ancient Near East, and its use in the Old Testament, see F. M. Cross, *Canaanite Myth and the Hebrew Epic* (Cambridge, Mass.: Harvard University Press, 1973), especially parts 2 and 3; P. D. Miller, Jr., *The Divine Warrior in Early Israel* (Cambridge, Mass.: Harvard University Press, 1973); and J. Jeremias, *Das Königtum*.

13. Exodus 15:1–18 is the parade example of this scenario and furnishes a full paradigm for the others. When the horizon of inquiry is the canon, it stands as introductory to all other cases in the psalms and elsewhere.

14. R. J. Clifford distinguishes between "cosmogonic" and "historic" types of Israel's national story, depending on the relative prominence of the human and the divine action and of the earthly and the heavenly perspective in *Fair-Spoken and Persuading* (Ramsay, N.J.: Paulist Press, 1984), 18ff.

15. J. L. Mays, "In a Vision: The Portrayal of the Messiah in the Psalms," in *Ex Auditu* 6 (1991): 1–8.

16. J. L. Mays, "The Place of the Torah-Psalms in the Psalter," *Journal of Biblical Literature* 106/1 (1987): 3–12.

## 3. Reading the Prayers in the Psalter

1. See Karl Barth, *Church Dogmatics*, II/2 (Edinburgh: T. & T. Clark, 1957), 719–21.

2. Martin Luther, *Luther's Works*, vol. 14 (St. Louis: Concordia Publishing House, 1974), 257.

3. John Calvin, *Commentary on the Book of Psalms*, vol. 4 (Edinburgh: Calvin Translation Society, 1847), 274ff.

4. Ibid., vol. 2, 272.

## 5. A Question of Identity

1. John Calvin, *Commentary on the Book of Psalms*, vol. 1 (Edinburgh: Calvin Translation Society, 1845), xxxiii.

2. Isaac Bashevis Singer, quoted in E. H. Peterson, *Answering God: The Psalms as Tools for Prayer* (San Francisco: Harper & Row, 1989), 36.

## 6. Hear Me, Help Me

1. Martin Luther, quoted in J. J. Stewart Perowne, *The Book of Psalms*, vol. 1 (Andover, Mass.: Warren F. Draper, 1898; repr. as *Commentary on the Psalms*, 2 vols. in 1, Grand Rapids: Kregel Publications, 1989), 156.

## 7. Praise Is Fitting

1. As printed in *The Presbyterian Hymnal* (Louisville, Ky.: Westminster/John Knox Press, 1990), no. 220.

2. As quoted by Geoffrey Wainwright from Homily 25.3 on Matthew, PG 57.331 in "The Praise of God in the Theological Reflection of the Church," *Interpretation* 39/1 (January 1985): 40.

3. Found in Douglas J. Hall, *Imaging God* (Grand Rapids: Wm. B. Eerdmans Publishing Co., 1986), 204.

4. John Calvin, *Commentary on the Book of Psalms*, vol. 1 (Edinburgh: Calvin Translation Society, 1845), 538.

5. Wainwright, "The Praise of God," 40.

6. Karl Barth, *Church Dogmatics*, III/4 (Edinburgh: T. & T. Clark, 1961), 73–86.

7. Ibid., 74.

8. Psalms 115; 135.

9. Brian Wren, *What Language Shall I Borrow? God-Talk in Worship* (New York: Crossroad, 1989), 124.

10. The source of the quotation is Edmund Steimle, in a sermon I cannot locate.

11. Tom Wright, *New Tasks for a Renewed Church* (London: Hodder & Stoughton, 1992), chaps. 8–10.

12. H. Gunkel, *Die Psalmen*, Göttinger Handkommentar zum Alten Testament II/2 (Göttingen: Vandenhoeck & Ruprecht, 1925), 431.

13. H.-J. Kraus, *The Theology of the Psalms* (Minneapolis: Augsburg Publishing House, 1986), 14.

14. Psalms 6, 30, 88, 115.

15. From *The Presbyterian Hymnal*, no. 253.

## 8. Worship, World, and Power

1. Manuscript evidence is divided between *Ketib* (*welo'* = "and not") and *Qere* (*welo* = "and his"). The Masora, which numbers it among the fifteen passages in which

*lo'* = *lo*, is generally followed by most moderns, but M. Dahood (*Psalms 51—100*, Anchor Bible [Garden City, N.Y.: Doubleday & Co., 1968], 371) prefers the *Ketib*, construed as a substantive ("nothing"). But both the symmetry of the parallel cola and usage (e.g., Ps. 95:5) support the *Qere*, and the proposal only saves the consonantal text at the cost of a construction that makes better sense in poetry and meaning.

2. For a résumé of its use in the liturgy of synagogue and church, see A. F. Kirkpatrick, *The Book of Psalms* (Cambridge: Cambridge University Press, 1912), 587f.

3. Much of the psalm is indeed woven of the "standard" words and phrases of Israel's cultic vocabulary. Verses 4 and 5 are a revision of the familiar *Todah*-hymn (see n. 8 below). The verbs represent the usual acts of worship: "Acclaim Yahweh" (Pss. 98:4, 6; 47:1; 66:1; etc.); "come, enter his presence, gates, courts" (95:6; 96:8); "bless him," "bless his name" (66:8; 96:2; 134:1f.; and so on); "thanksgiving," "mirth," "joyous shout," "praise" are common. The brief treatment given Ps. 100 in most commentaries is probably due to its position after Pss. 95 and 98, which contain sections of identical text.

4. Hermann Gunkel protests that Ps. 100 should not be too highly valued, since it does not depart from the ordinary, though he admits it could have been the focus of an enthusiastic festival (*Die Psalmen*, Handkommentar zum Alten Testament, II/2, 4th ed. [Göttingen: Vandenhoeck & Ruprecht, 1926], 432).

5. H. Gunkel and J. Begrich, *Einleitung in die Psalmen*, Handkommentar zum Alten Testament (Göttingen: Vandenhoeck & Ruprecht, 1933), chap. 2, sec. 18. For the first element of the form, see chap. 2, secs. 6, 8. Examples of this version of the form (plural imperative summons plus declaration introduced by "for"): Pss. 9:11f.; 22:23f.; 30:4f.; 33:1–5; 47:1f., 6f.

6. Claus Westermann isolates a specific group of psalms, which he names "the Imperative Psalms" and among which he includes Ps. 100 (*The Praise of God in the Psalms* [Richmond: John Knox Press, 1965], 131). His analysis of the elements observes the function of v. 3 and hardly fits the other psalms cited with enough accuracy to establish a coherent group. Psalm 100 is certainly better understood as a variation on the *Todah* version of the old basic hymn form.

7. Ibid., sec. 7.7. See also K. Koch, "Denn seine Güte währet ewiglich," *Evangelische Theologie* 12 (1961): 531ff.

8. Psalms 106:1; 107:1; 118:1, 29; 136:1ff.; 1 Chron. 16:34; 2 Chron. 5:13; 7:3; Ezra 3:11.

9. See below, n. 13.

10. "Speaking precisely, the Psalm contains two hymns" (Gunkel's commentary, 432); "two short hymns" (H.-J. Kraus, *Psalmen*, Biblische Kommentar, 15 [Neukirchen-Vluyn: Neukirchener Verlag des Erziehungsvereins, 1960], 686).

11. The "type" was identified and discussed by W. Zimmerli in *Erkenntnis Gottes nach dem Buche Ezechiel*, Abhandlungen zur Theologie des Alten und Neuen Testaments, 27 (Zurich: Zwingli-Verlag, 1954), now in *Gottes Offenbarung*, Theologische Bücherei, 19 (Munich: Chr. Kaiser Verlag, 1963), 41ff. (pages cited according to the latter). See esp. 66–69.

12. Deuteronomy 4:39; 7:9; cf. 1 Kings 8:60; 2 Kings 19:19.

13. The universal reference is apparent in similar uses (Pss. 66:1; 96:1; 97:5, 9; 98:4).

14. The Köhler-Baumgartner *Lexicon* defines *'abad* in Ps. 100:2 and similar texts as "to worship a god, specifically, to perform his cult" (p. 671). This is correct, of course; the problem is the use the interpreter makes of the flag "cult."

15. *'abad* is surprisingly infrequent in the Psalter for a "cultic" term, and used always in relation to a royal figure (human or divine). "Serve Yahweh" occurs in the Psalter only at Ps. 2:11. See Pss. 18:43; 22:30; 72:11; 97:7; 102:22. The exception in 106:36 is only apparent.

16. Exodus 3:12; 4:23; 7:16; 8:1; 10:26.

17. Deuteronomy 7:4; 8:19; 11:16; 12:2, for example.

18. Before Saul (1 Sam. 10:24).

19. First Kings 1:28, 32.

20. The older commentators, noting the relation of Ps. 100 to the group of psalms, Pss. 93–99, that celebrate Yahweh's kingship, recognized this aspect. "If we are right in regarding Psalms xciii–xcix as forming one continuous series . . . whose title is 'Jehovah is King' . . . this Psalm may be regarded as the doxology which closes the refrain" (J.J.S. Perowne, *The Book of Psalms* [Andover, Mass.: Warren F. Draper, 1898], vol. 2, 203).

21. Note the imperative use of the formula in Ps. 46:10.

22. "Because the recognition expressed in the recognition-formula always follows the act of Yahweh, the command to 'know' can never be the primary assertion. Such a summons to recognition is possible only where Yahweh's action, even though it take the form of an authoritative pronouncement of his coming action, has become visible" (Zimmerli, *Erkenntnis Gottes*, 88).

23. For "make" as a metaphor for Yahweh's election and salvation, cf. Ps. 95:6f.; Deut. 32:6, 15; Isa. 43:1, 21; 44:2. The relation of the parallel pastoral image ("the flock he pastures") to the election of Yahweh is apparent in its use in the community lament: Pss. 74:1; 79:13. The metrical versions of Ps. 100 have pushed it away from its basis in Israel's knowledge of Yahweh through his particular deeds to a general theology of creation; they speak of "God" (not the LORD), take "make" to mean "create," and refer to "all blessings" in a summary sense.

24. On this point, see Westermann, *The Praise of God*, 25–30, and the literature there cited.

25. Ibid., 30.

26. Mark 10:18 and parallels.

27. Psalms 106; 136.

28. Psalm 118.

29. Psalm 107.

30. N. Glueck's basic study of 1927 is now available in English: *Hesed in the Bible* (Cincinnati: Hebrew Union College Press, 1967). G. A. Larue has added a valuable introductory survey of "Recent Studies in *hesed*," pp. 1–32.

## 9. The David of the Psalms

1. Babylonian Talmud *Pesaḥim* 117a.

2. Babylonian Talmud *Baba Batra* 14b.

3. See the texts cited in G. Friedrich, ed., *Theological Dictionary of the New Testament*, vol. 8 (Grand Rapids: Wm. B. Eerdmans Publishing Co., 1972), 487.

4. On matters in this paragraph, see J. A. Sanders, *The Dead Sea Psalms Scroll* (Ithaca, N.Y.: Cornell University Press, 1967). The numbering of psalms from the scroll is that given by Sanders.

5. P. Kyle McCarter, Jr., *I Samuel*, Anchor Bible, vol. 8 (Garden City, N.Y.: Doubleday & Co., 1980), 282.

6. E. Werner, "Music," *Interpreter's Dictionary of the Bible*, vol. 3 (Nashville: Abingdon Press, 1962), 457.

7. In verses 14 and 16, McCarter corrects "dancing with all his might" to "strumming on sonorous instruments." P. Kyle McCarter, Jr., *II Samuel*, Anchor Bible, vol. 9 (Garden City, N.Y.: Doubleday & Co., 1984), 162.

8. On this and other matters in this section, see N. M. Sarna, "The Psalm Superscriptions and the Guilds," in *Studies in Jewish Religious and Intellectual History*, ed. S. Stein and R. Loewe (University, Ala.: University of Alabama Press, 1979), 281–300.

9. On the titles of these psalms and their implications, see the seminal analysis of Brevard S. Childs, "Psalm Titles and Midrashic Exegesis," *Journal of Semitic Studies* 16 (1971): 137–50.

## 10. "In a Vision"

1. The title, "In a Vision," comes from a significant location, Ps. 89:19.

2. Reinhold Niebuhr, *The Nature and Destiny of Man*, vol. 2 (New York: Charles Scribner's Sons, 1946), 15.

3. Wolfhart Pannenberg, *Jesus—God and Man* (Philadelphia: Westminster Press, 1977), 32.

## 12. Going by the Book

1. The following may be consulted. The chapter on Psalms in Brevard S. Childs, *Introduction to the Old Testament as Scripture* (Philadelphia: Fortress Press, 1979), is the initial impulse. The basic work on the form and formation of the Psalter is G. H. Wilson, *The Editing of the Hebrew Psalter* (Chico, Calif.: Scholars Press, 1985). The essays collected in J. Clinton McCann, ed., *The Shape and Shaping of the Psalter* (Sheffield: JSOT Press, 1993), give a good representation of work on the subject. See also the essays in *Interpretation*, April 1992. All of the above have been helpful in composing the present chapter.

2. For a commentary that is paying sustained attention to the arrangement of the psalms as a factor in their interpretation, see F.-L. Hossfeld and E. Zenger, *Die Psalmen I* (Psalms 1—50) in the series *Die Neue Echter Bibel* (Würzburg: Echter Verlag, 1993).

3. On presence and pervasiveness of the torah theme in the Psalter, see "The Place of the Torah Psalms in the Psalter," chapter 13 in this volume.

4. See "The Center of the Psalms," chapter 2 in this volume.

5. On the entire question of David and the Psalms, see "The David of the Psalms," chapter 9 in this volume.

6. On the psalms that describe the anointed king see " 'In a Vision': The Portrayal of the Messiah in the Psalms," chapter 10 in this volume.

7. G. H. Wilson has argued persuasively that the "royal psalms" have been used for strategic purposes at the seams between the first three and the fourth books of the Psalter. See his "The Use of the Royal Psalms at the 'Seams' of the Hebrew Psalter," *Journal for the Study of the Old Testament* 35 (1986): 85–94.

## 13. The Place of the Torah Psalms in the Psalter

1. For an orientation to approaching Psalms as a book, see Brevard S. Childs, *Introduction to the Old Testament as Scripture* (Philadelphia: Fortress Press, 1979), chap. 33.

2. For a somewhat similar assessment of these connections, see P. D. Miller, Jr., *Interpreting the Psalms* (Philadelphia: Fortress Press, 1986), 83–84.

3. M. Fishbane, "Psalm 19: Creation, Torah, and Hope," in *Text and Texture* (New York: Schocken Books, 1979), 84–90. D.J.A. Clines, "The Tree of Knowledge and the Law of Yahweh (Psalm XIX)," *Vetus Testamentum* 24 (1974): 8–14.

4. See the excellent assessment of H. Gunkel's *Mischgattungen* in F. Stolz, *Psalmen im nachkultischen Raum*, Theologische Studien, 129 (Zurich: Theologischer Verlag, 1983), 23–27.

5. I am using "torah" as a comprehensive term for what is named discursively by the cluster of nouns in Ps. 19 (*'edut, piqqudim, miṣwa, yir'ah, mišpaṭim*) and in Ps. 119 (*'edot/'edwot, piqqudim, dabar, mišpaṭim, miṣwot, huqqim, 'imrah, derek, 'oraḥ*), and giving the RSV's translations, since they are familiar and none is entirely satisfactory, though note what the Jewish Publication Society version has done. *Torah* when translated is "instruction, teaching," and "law" is avoided for well-known reasons.

6. J. Becker, *Gottesfurcht im alten Testament*, Analecta Biblica 25 (Rome: Pontifical Biblical Institute, 1965), 268–74.

7. H.-J. Hermisson, *Sprache und Ritus im altisraelitischen Kult. Zur Spiritualisierung der Kultbegriff im Alten Testament* (Wissenschaftliche Monographien zum Alten und Neuen Testament, 19; Neukirchen-Vluyn: Neukirchener Verlag, 1965). S. Towner makes the same point about the prayer in Daniel 9 in "Retributional Theology in the Apocalyptic Setting," *Union Seminary Quarterly Review* (1971): 203–14.

8. A. Deissler, *Psalm 119 (118) und seine Theologie* (Münchener Theologische Studien, I/2; Munich, 1955), an exhaustive study of the psalm and its relation to other psalms and Hebrew scriptures, is the basic resource for any study of Psalm 119.

9. It is not the appearance of single terms so much as their collocation in clusters of two or more that is the issue. See the useful table showing the composition and location of clusters in G. Liedke, *Gestalt und Bezeichnung alttestamentlicher Rechtssätze* (WMANT, 39; Neukirchen-Vluyn: Neukirchener Verlag, 1971), 11–18.

10. A. Deissler, *Psalm 119(118)*, 270–80.

11. Note the use of *siah, daraš, lamad, sipper* in the psalm.

12. Psalms 18, 25, 33, 78, 89, 93, 94, 99, 103, 105, 111, 112, 147, 148.

13. For a study of the connection of the texts with prophetic books, see H.-J. Kraus, "Zum Gesetzesverständnis der nachprophetischen Zeit," in *Biblische-Theologische Aufsätze* (Neukirchen-Vluyn: Neukirchener Verlag, 1972), 278–95.

14. Note *hagah* in Pss. 1:2; 37:30; *hegyon* in 19:15 and also the verbs in note 11.

15. See especially G. T. Sheppard, *Wisdom as a Hermeneutical Construct*, Beihefte zur Zeitschrift für Alttestamentliche Wissenschaft, 151 (Berlin: Walter de Gruyter, 1980), 136–43.

16. Among others, see Childs, *Introduction*, 517–18; C. Westermann, *Praise and Lament in the Psalms* (Atlanta: John Knox Press, 1981), 258.

17. On Pss. 111/112 and 105/106 see W. Zimmerli, "Zwillingspsalmen," in *Studien zur alttestamentlichen Theologie und Prophetie*, Theologische Bücherei, Altes Testament, 51 (Munich: Chr. Kaiser Verlag, 1974), 261–71.

## 14. Psalm 118 in the Light
## of Canonical Analysis

1. Brevard S. Childs, *Introduction to the Old Testament as Scripture* (Philadelphia: Fortress Press, 1979).

2. Brevard S. Childs, *Biblical Theology in Crisis* (Philadelphia: Westminster Press, 1970); *The Book of Exodus*, Old Testament Library (Philadelphia: Westminster Press, 1974).

3. Sentences from Childs, *Introduction*, 83.

4. Hermann Gunkel, *Die Psalmen*, Handkommentar zum Alten Testament, II/2, 4th ed. (Göttingen: Vandenhoeck & Ruprecht, 1926), 504ff.

5. Sigmund Mowinckel, *The Psalms in Israel's Worship*, vol. 1 (Oxford: Basil Blackwell Publisher, 1962), 180–81.

6. For a convenient summary of recent work on Ps. 118, see Leslie C. Allen, *Psalms 101—150*, Word Biblical Commentary, 21 (Waco, Tex.: Word Books, 1983), 122–25.

7. See esp. chap. 33 on "The Psalms," in Childs, *Introduction*.

8. See Childs, *Introduction*, 84–103.

9. Note Childs's emphasis on "the community of faith and practice which preserved and shaped it" as the historical setting of scripture (*Introduction*, 41, 71, 73, 76, 77, 83). He insists that canonical analysis is a *descriptive* task, which holds the language of the Old Testament within the interpretive context of historic Israel, even though canon frees the texts from the past. What Childs means by "historic Israel" and a "community of faith and practice" is somewhat elusive, but it becomes an issue in working with a particular passage. Is exegesis also a *descriptive* task? The remarks on page 83 of *Introduction* leave uncertainty. This chapter is written on the assumption that exegesis also should be descriptive.

10. For the first, see J. Becker, *Israel deutet seine Psalmen*, Stuttgarter Bibelstudien, 18 (Stuttgart: Katholisches Bibelwerk, 1966), 56–57. For the second, compare the interpretation in A. Deissler, *Die Psalmen* (Düsseldorf: Patmos Verlag, 1964).

# Bibliographical Postscript

The books identified in the following list were selected on the basis of two criteria. First, they are resources that I have used and found useful in studying the psalms with theological students and ministers. Second, they are a selection that fits the approach and topics of the chapters in this volume. Comprehensive bibliographies are available in every introduction to the Psalms and to the Old Testament, and in every standard critical commentary.

There are two good introductions to the critical study of the psalms. Klaus Seybold, *Introducing the Psalms* (Edinburgh: T & T. Clark, 1990), covers all aspects of contemporary psalm study and includes chapters on the use and interpretation of psalms. *Psalms*, by J. Day, in the Old Testament Guides series (Sheffield: JSOT Press, 1990) gives a good overview and assessment of current positions on the major questions of psalm criticism.

One introductory book deserves its own paragraph: Claus Westermann, *Praise and Lament in the Psalms* (Atlanta: John Knox Press, 1981). The book is a form-critical interpretation of the psalms, which has the very special virtue of demonstrating the theological potential of form criticism. The smaller *The Psalms: Structure, Content and Message* (Minneapolis: Augsburg Publishing House, 1980) is a compact version of *Praise and Lament in the Psalms*.

There are also introductory works concerned more directly with the use of the psalms and addressed to a general audience. Patrick D. Miller, Jr., *Interpreting the Psalms* (Philadelphia: Fortress Press, 1986), combines essays on major aspects of psalm interpretation with a set of expository essays on an illustrative group of psalms. Roland E. Murphy, *The Psalms Are Yours* (Mahwah, N.J.: Paulist Press, 1993), contains a perceptive, judicious review of introductory matters and a brief commentary on the psalms, all in 148 pages. J. Clinton McCann, Jr., *A Theological Introduction to the Book of Psalms* (Nashville: Abingdon Press, 1993), is oriented to the recent concern with psalms as part of a book. There are chapters on the different functions of psalms, composed of expositions of specific texts.

For exegetical commentaries on the Hebrew text, I recommend the two-volume work by Hans-Joachim Kraus: vol. I, *Psalms 1–59;* vol. II, *Psalms 60–150* (Minneapolis: Augsburg Fortress, 1987, 1989); and volumes 19, 20, and 21 in the Word Biblical Commentary (Waco, Tex.: Word Books), by Peter C. Craigie (1983), Marvin E. Tate (1991), and L. C. Allen (1983). Artur Weiser's *The Psalms, A Commentary,* in the Old Testament Library (Philadelphia: Westminster Press, 1962) is another good resource in one volume.

Two expository commentaries should be noted. Walter Brueggemann, *The Message of the Psalms* (Minneapolis: Augsburg Publishing House, 1984), is termed by the author "a post-critical reading" that combines the theological purpose of traditional interpretation with the approach of critical scholarship. Then there is my volume on *Psalms* in the Interpretation series to which this book is a companion (Louisville, Ky.: John Knox Press, 1994); its plan is oriented to the classic and current uses of psalms in the church.

Older works often offer insights and put a psalm in a perspective lost in contemporary study. The commentaries of Franz Delitzsch (repr. Grand Rapids: Wm. B. Eerdmans Publishing Co., 1980) and J. J. Stewart Perowne (Andover, Mass.: Warren F. Draper, 1898; repr. Grand Rapids: Kregel Publications, 1989) have always proved rewarding when consulted.

Nothing enhances one's appreciation of the richness of meaning in psalms more than a journey through the history of their interpretation and use. One way to take the journey is with the help of a guide. William L. Holladay, *The Psalms through Three Thousand Years* (Minneapolis: Fortress Press, 1993), provides a tour that begins with Israel and concludes with the contemporary scene. Quite a different route is offered by Rowland E. Prothero, *The Psalms in History and Biography* (New York: Robert Carter, 1886), a little history of the church composed of quotes and anecdotal accounts of the use of the psalms in every era. Yet another way is to see how a psalm is understood in the classic milieus. The route could go through these stations: William G. Braude, *The Midrash on Psalms,* 2 vols. (New Haven, Conn.: Yale University Press, 1959); James M. Neale and Richard F. Littledale, *A Commentary on the Psalms from Primitive and Medieval Writers,* 4 vols. (London: Masters, 1860–83); *Luther's Works,* vols. 10–14 (St. Louis: Concordia Publishing House, 1974–76 and 1955–58); John Calvin, *Commentary on the Book of Psalms,* 5 vols. (Edinburgh: Calvin Translation Society, 1845–49).

Expository writing and essays on particular psalms constitute another helpful resource for the interpreter. One will find stimulating but different approaches in these works: Martin Buber, *Right and Wrong* (London: SCM Press, 1952): C. S. Lewis, *Reflections on the Psalms* (New York: Harcourt, Brace & Co., 1958): James Limburg, *Psalms for Sojourners* (Minneapolis: Augsburg Publishing House, 1986); Nathan M. Sarna, *Songs of the Heart* (New York: Schocken Books, 1993). The journal *Interpretation* publishes expository essays on biblical texts in each issue; a psalm is the text chosen from time to time. Some works that do not quite fit in the above groups are important. There are two scholars whose seminal work is basic for all who work in psalms study, Hermann Gunkel and Sigmund Mowinckel. It is a true irony of publication history that Gunkel's great *Einleitung in die Psalmen* (1933) and his commentary *Die Psalmen* (1926) have never been translated. But one can read Mowinckel's *The Psalms in Israel's Worship*, 2 vols. (Oxford: Basil Blackwell Publisher, 1962), for his foundational attempt to locate the psalms in precise cultic contexts. Othmar Keel's *The Symbolism of the Biblical World: Ancient Near Eastern Iconography and the Book of Psalms* (New York: Crossroad, 1985) is an invaluable guide to the participation of the psalms in the culture of the ancient Near East. Hans-Joachim Kraus, *Theology of the Psalms* (Minneapolis: Augsburg Publishing House, 1986), a companion to his commentary, is the only available full-scale theology of the psalms.

Of the numerous books on the psalms as prayer, these should be listed: Dietrich Bonhoeffer, *Psalms, The Prayer Book of the Bible* (Minneapolis: Augsburg Publishing House, 1970); Walter Brueggemann, *Praying the Psalms* (Winona, Minn.: St. Mary's Press, 1982); Eugene H. Peterson, *Answering God: The Psalms as Tools for Prayer* (San Francisco: Harper & Row, 1989). Walter Brueggemann, *Israel's Praise: Doxology against Idolatry and Ideology* (Philadelphia: Fortress Press, 1988), is a stimulating treatment of the psalms for praise from the perspective of a liberation theology hermeneutic.

Though they cannot be adequately accounted for in a bibliography, liturgical materials constitute one of the richest resources for psalm interpretation. Lectionaries locate psalms in the contexts of seasons and other lections. Hymnals provide metrical psalms and highly interpretive hymnic versions of psalms. Worship books and choral renditions propose readings of psalms that elicit special dimensions in them.

At the conclusion of this list of works on the psalms, let it be said that the first and primary resource for psalm interpretation is the psalms themselves. The way to discover their true worth as scripture and liturgy is to read, meditate on, pray, and sing the psalms.

# Index of
# Passages Discussed